Stretching for Seniors

Daily Mobility Exercises and Stretches to Increase Flexibility, Improve Posture, and Prevent Injury

© Copyright 2023 - All rights reserved.

The content contained within this book may not be reproduced, duplicated, or transmitted without direct written permission from the author or the publisher.

Under no circumstances will any blame or legal responsibility be held against the publisher, or author, for any damages, reparation, or monetary loss due to the information contained within this book, either directly or indirectly.

Legal Notice:

This book is copyright protected. It is only for personal use. You cannot amend, distribute, sell, use, quote, or paraphrase any part, or the content within this book, without the consent of the author or publisher.

Disclaimer Notice:

Please note the information contained within this document is for educational and entertainment purposes only. All effort has been executed to present accurate, up-to-date, reliable, and complete information. No warranties of any kind are declared or implied. Readers acknowledge that the author is not engaging in the rendering of legal, financial, medical, or professional advice. The content within this book has been derived from various sources. Please consult a licensed professional before attempting any techniques outlined in this book.

By reading this document, the reader agrees that under no circumstances is the author responsible for any losses, direct or indirect, that are incurred as a result of the use of the information contained within this document, including, but not limited to, errors, omissions, or inaccuracies.

Free Bonuses from Scott Hamrick

Hi seniors!

My name is Scott Hamrick, and first off, I want to THANK YOU for reading my book.

Now you have a chance to join my exclusive "workout for seniors" email list so you can get the ebook below for free as well as the potential to get more ebooks for seniors for free! Simply click the link below to join.

P.S. Remember that it's 100% free to join the list.

Access your free bonuses here
https://livetolearn.lpages.co/scott-hamrick-stretching-for-seniors-paperback/

Table of Contents

FREE BONUSES FROM SCOTT HAMRICK 5
INTRODUCTION: 1
CHAPTER 1: WHY SHOULD I STRETCH? 3
CHAPTER 2: MORNING STRETCHES 17
CHAPTER 3: EVENING STRETCHES 26
CHAPTER 4: CORE EXERCISES & STRETCHING 35
CHAPTER 5: ROUTINES FOR DAILY ACTIVITY 49
CHAPTER 6: PINPOINT FOCUS: THE HIPS 78
CHAPTER 7: PINPOINT FOCUS: NECK AND SHOULDERS 84
CHAPTER 8: PINPOINT FOCUS: KNEES, ANKLES & FEET 89
CHAPTER 9: STRETCHING PROPERLY 101
CHAPTER 10: UPPING YOUR GAME 110
HERE'S ANOTHER BOOK BY SCOTT HAMRICK THAT YOU MIGHT LIKE 137
FREE BONUSES FROM SCOTT HAMRICK 138

Introduction:

On average, people in their 30s have a range of motion of 14% in their joints. But that number drops significantly in older adults with a range of motion of only 5.2%! The loss of flexibility is caused by the wear and tear of joints and muscles as the body ages.

Performing tasks becomes more challenging, and muscles feel tight and stiff. Enjoying retirement (as you planned out in your head) may not be progressing as you had previously thought. You have all this time but feel your body is preventing you from doing the things you always wanted to do.

It becomes harder to stay active, and sitting on the couch seems like the best and least painful option. But here is where the never-ending loop starts: the less you stay active, the more your body cages you inside.

And the harder it is to get up and enjoy life. Suddenly, you realize that your quality of life has gone south. Anger gets a hold of you, and you can't blame anything other than *the curse of old age.*

But what if old age isn't the thing that is doing this to you? Let's take John as an example. John loves food, and he just can't help it. Every morning, he wakes up and decides what he wants to order. In the evening, he eats yet another order of takeout.

After several months, not only have his meals gotten big enough to feed a family, but John also gained 65 pounds. When he realizes this, he gets angry. Angry at food. Food has ruined his life and has made him addicted. If only his appetite were less strong, his life would be normal...

But John doesn't understand that throughout these months, he has expanded and trained his stomach to hold more food. He has also trained his brain to send out hunger signals more frequently. Food is not the problem; it is an essential fuel on which to live.

John is the problem. His body is treating him the same way he is treating his body – which cannot be truer for older adults. It's not the age that keeps you sore and stiff, and it's how you surrender to old age, just like John surrendered to food.

All of us are blessed with medicine that cures and prevents thousands of age-related conditions. This medicine is found within us, and it is activated *the more we pursue it.* It's called physical activity. People fail to realize that just a few minutes of even the lightest of physical activity will completely change your life – from how you handle stress to how you socialize and even how you feel. Regaining your stamina back might seem like a laughable topic. But what if it was true?

What if you could feel 30 again just by starting to add a few minutes of stretches to your daily routine? You might be either laughing at this or are deeply interested as to how this can be possible.

Either way, you have nothing to lose. This book is entirely dedicated to how you can gain complete control of your life by stretching your body. The following chapters will give a broad introduction to stretching and how you can use it to ease muscle pain, stiffness, soreness, and tiredness, and just enjoy the things you always wanted to do without overthinking your health.

Reminder: This book aims to educate readers about the benefits of stretching. Do NOT take the context of this book as a way to cure illnesses or medical diagnoses. The reader is not advised to use this book as a way to self-diagnose or self-treat themselves. Talk to your doctor about adding stretching to your daily routine, changing your diet, or if you think you are suffering from an undiagnosed condition.

Chapter 1: Why Should I Stretch?

Stretching has been practiced for thousands of years, beginning with martial arts and yoga practitioners. In the early 20th century, it was promoted as a way to keep military personnel physically fit during training. It has also been practiced to improve flexibility by dancers and gymnasts. Stretching has now become an accepted part of physical fitness regimens. It has also been incorporated into therapeutic practices designed to relieve pain.

It's one of the best ways to improve your health and well-being. Stretching your body reduces stiffness in the joints, helps maintain mobility and flexibility, relieves muscle soreness, improves blood circulation, and alleviates stress. It's also an excellent way to prepare your body for exercise. Stretching exercises can help improve posture, balance, and strength as well as reduce feelings of stiffness. The practice has been a part of athletes' training regimens for decades.

One study published in the Journal of Aging Research found that physically active seniors have better physical function than those who are inactive. They also found that stretching exercises helped improve balance, which is essential for preventing falls among older adults. If you're a senior, adding stretching exercises to your daily routine might significantly improve your quality of life.

Stretching increases the range of motion in your joints by lengthening muscle fibers without causing injury or pain. This helps maintain flexibility as you age and reduces the risk of arthritis and other joint problems later in life. Stretching also improves heart health and is vital for performing daily tasks and athletic activities such as running or jumping.

Regular stretching increases blood flow through your veins and arteries, which improves circulation throughout your body and helps remove waste products from cells. Increasing circulation also increases oxygenation to muscles, which helps prevent muscle cramps during exercise or everyday tasks such as walking upstairs or carrying groceries from the car into the house after grocery shopping.

The study, published in the Journal of Strength and Conditioning Research, focused on the effect of stretching before and after exercise. Flexibility is important for all individuals but especially important for older adults.

The study randomly assigned 40 women aged 65-77 to either a stretching group or a control group that did not participate in any extra exercises. Both groups received supervised training sessions three times a week for 24 weeks. The stretching group performed static stretches before each training session. In contrast, the control group did not perform any extra stretches before starting their training program.

The results showed that both groups improved their flexibility over time; however, those in the stretching group increased their flexibility more than those in the control group (an average increase of 2%).

Muscles that aren't as flexible can become tight from repetitive use or sitting in one position for long periods. Stretching helps relieve this tightness, allowing you to move more easily and comfortably. One study published in Medicine & Science in Sports & Exercise found that people who did balance training and stretching fell fewer times than those who didn't do balance training after six months.

Another fantastic benefit of stretching is that it helps you relax by releasing endorphins in your body. These endorphins have been proven to help reduce stress levels and improve overall well-being.

A study by Dr. Herbert Benson at Harvard Medical School showed that people who practiced daily meditation and stretching showed lowered heart rates, lower blood pressure, and lower levels of cortisol (the stress hormone). It also resulted in improved immune function, better sleep quality, and less pain sensitivity.

Stretching can even help with pain management. This helps reduce pain associated with muscle spasms or soreness from working out too hard or playing sports too aggressively.

Good posture, on the other hand, is essential for maintaining healthy back muscles and joints – especially as you age – but it's often difficult to achieve daily due to factors such as stress at work or home life, poor sleep habits, and improper nutrition habits (e.g., eating high-fat foods). Stretching your body might help you with improving your posture.

If you have trouble sleeping at night, stretching before bedtime may help you relax and fall asleep faster. It's also good for your heart because it can lower blood pressure and reduce the risk of developing heart disease or stroke. You can stretch at any time, but it's best to do so before or after a workout, at bedtime, or first thing in the morning. Here are some of the most common types of stretching:

Static stretching

Static stretching is a form of stretching in which you hold the stretch for a certain period of time. The person doing the static stretch holds an extended position while his or her muscles are stretched to their limit. They are usually held for 10 to 30 seconds.

This kind of stretching is sometimes called passive stretching because it's done in a relaxed manner and not with a lot of movement. This can reduce the risk of injury and make day-to-day activities easier.

It also helps to loosen up tight muscles and connective tissues, which improves circulation and reduces pain in your joints. It even increases the elasticity of your muscles, allowing them to stretch farther than they would normally be able to without injury. This can improve performance during exercise or sport and make everyday activities easier on your body.

Static stretches are also helpful for lengthening your muscles and tendons so that they don't pull too short when you move them through their full range of motion. The less painful it is for you to move through these ranges, the better off you'll be!

Dynamic stretching

Dynamic stretching is flexibility training that uses smooth, continuous movements to improve the body's daily performance. It can help prevent injury by warming up muscles before exercise and increasing blood flow to muscles. It also helps improve performance by loosening stiff joints.

Dynamic stretching is different from static stretching, which mainly targets the muscles' length (how far they can stretch), as it also targets the muscle's ability to contract through a full range of motion. Dynamic stretching is a great way for seniors to warm up before any type of physical activity.

Here are some of the benefits you'll enjoy when you do these stretches:

Increased blood flow: It increases blood flow to your muscles and joints, which helps them function properly.

Improved balance and coordination: Dynamic stretching improves your balance and coordination by increasing your muscles' strength, power, and endurance. This can help prevent falls and other accidents in older adults who have reduced balance because of age or illness.

Enhanced performance: It improves athletic performance by increasing overall body coordination, flexibility, and speed while improving muscle control.

Ballistic stretching

Ballistic stretching is a type of active stretching that uses momentum to lengthen the muscle. It's done by bouncing or throwing your body into the stretch, which usually creates tension in the muscle.

Ballistic stretching is a type of active isolated stretching. This should not be confused with ballistic exercises such as plyometrics. This stretching involves performing an explosive movement when stretching a muscle or group of muscles. This is in contrast to static stretching, which involves holding a stretch for 10 to 30 seconds.

Ballistic stretches are particularly useful for increasing range of motion in the hip flexors and quadriceps, often looser in seniors due to lack of use. In addition, ballistic stretching can help improve joint flexibility and muscle elasticity and reduce muscle stiffness caused by sitting for long periods.

It should be performed after warming up your body through dynamic exercises such as jogging on the spot or doing jumping jacks. Perform each stretch slowly and gently until you feel resistance from the target muscle group. Then explosively stretch that muscle until you feel your muscles relax again.

The vast majority of studies on stretching have been done on static stretching. While there are some benefits to static stretching, it can also be harmful and cause injury. A study published in the Journal of Strength and Conditioning Research found that static stretching before exercising reduced power output by 8.3 percent during leg exercises. Static stretching also decreased muscle strength by 3 to 5 percent in these exercises.

This kind of stretching is generally not recommended before exercise because it can reduce your ability to perform physical activity at full capacity, according to another study published in the International Journal of Sports Sciences and Medicine (IJSSM). The study found that static-only stretching caused more muscle damage than no stretching before high-intensity workouts such as cycling sprints or resistance training.

Dynamic stretching is a more effective form of warm-up than static stretching because it prepares your muscles for movement without decreasing their power output or strength levels. It also allows you to move through exercises more easily without straining yourself or risking an injury.

It's important to note that stretching is not exactly the same as warming up. Warm-ups help prepare your body for physical activity by increasing blood flow and preparing muscles to work harder. Stretching is a more passive activity that focuses on lengthening muscles, tendons, ligaments, and other connective tissue before the workout.

Still, the two remain highly similar and constantly get confused. It is recommended to warm up the body first and then perform a series of dynamic stretches before exercising.

Here are five tips for keeping your stretching safe as you age:

1. Avoid overhead stretches in which you raise your arms above shoulder height. This can cause compression in the cervical spine, leading to pinched nerves in the neck and shoulders.

2. Avoid twisting movements that involve rotating your head while keeping your torso still. Twisting too much can cause stress injuries in the low back and hip joints, while rotating the head too far can harm nerves in the neck.

3. Don't push yourself too hard when stretching—this could lead to muscle tears and other injuries that may even require surgery down the road. It's better to start slow and gradually increase your flexibility than rush into exercises that might hurt you in the long run!

4. Stretching should not hurt. If you feel any pain while stretching, stop immediately and consult a doctor before attempting it again (or try another stretch altogether). Pain is a sign that something is not right.

5. Warm up before you stretch. A warm-up will help increase blood flow to your muscles and reduce their risk of injury during stretching. Try walking around the house for five minutes before stretching, then start by doing some light stretches before doing more advanced moves.

Stretching exercises should be done regularly (daily) because our bodies constantly change throughout life. As we age, our bodies change shape over time due to gravity, stress, and other factors. By keeping our muscles flexible and loose through stretching, we can prevent injury and improve circulation to our spine, which helps keep us healthy overall!

Yoga vs. stretching: What is the difference?

Yoga and stretching are two physical activities that are often confused. Both practices improve flexibility, relieve stress, and strengthen the body. However, distinct differences between both practices make each of them unique.

Yoga is an ancient science that has been practiced for thousands of years. It is a system of self-improvement and spiritual growth through body, mind, and spirit development. Yoga involves conscious breathing techniques, physical postures (asanas), and meditation (dhyana).

The word *yoga* comes from the Sanskrit word Yuj, which means "to join" or "to unite." Yoga teaches us how to join our body, mind, and spirit to live in harmony with ourselves and others.

The word *asana* comes from the Sanskrit root *asan,* which means "seat," referring to sitting in meditation postures. Yoga asanas are exercises that help develop strength, flexibility, balance, and concentration. They make you feel good physically as well as mentally and spiritually.

Yoga postures are not just physical movements but also mental exercises that bring about relaxation and calmness by helping us focus on one thing at a time instead of many things at once. This helps us reach higher levels of consciousness where we can experience inner peace and tranquility, which is what yoga really is all about!

The practice is believed to have been composed as early as the third century B.C. The most famous text of classical yoga is Patañjali's Yoga Sūtras, but many other texts also contribute to its formation. Yoga can also be considered a philosophy promoted by Hindu religious groups as an essential element of their religion.

Yogis believe that you can experience greater spiritual growth when you're physically and mentally relaxed. Stretchers often focus on the physical aspects of their workouts, so they don't always achieve this kind of mental relaxation.

Yoga has been gaining popularity in the US for years now, but it seems like it's becoming even more mainstream these days. There are yoga studios everywhere, and every city has at least one studio that offers classes for all levels.

Yoga is a great way to de-stress, get in shape, and stretch your body. It also has many mental health benefits, like reducing anxiety and depression, making you happier, and improving memory. The popularity of yoga has grown so much that people have started doing it outside of their normal class time as well. The trend seems to be called "yoga on the fly" or "yoga anywhere." This means that people often do sun salutations or other poses outside of their usual yoga class or studio.

While this doesn't seem like a big deal at first glance, it's actually quite dangerous because some poses require instructor supervision to be done safely without injuring yourself. Also, many nuances can only be shown by an instructor who knows what they're doing, so if you're not careful, you could end up hurting yourself while trying to do something on your own without any guidance from someone who knows how it should be done properly.

Stretching, on the other hand, is a form of exercise designed to increase muscle flexibility by elongating muscles past their normal range of motion. Stretchers typically hold each stretch for about 30 seconds before releasing it and repeating the stretch several times over an extended period of time (usually several minutes). Stretching should never cause pain or discomfort – if you feel pain during any stretch, stop immediately before further damage occurs!

One similarity between yoga and stretching is that they both involve physical activity that can be done at home or at the gym. Both types of exercise have been around for centuries and have been used by many different cultures worldwide.

The ancient Greeks did exercises similar to yoga during meditation to relax their bodies and minds. Stretching has also been used since ancient times as a way for people to stay flexible throughout their lives to perform tasks more easily without injury or pain later on in life.

Another similarity between these two exercises is that there are many different types of each, so you can choose one that fits your needs best, whether you want more flexibility or relaxation. Stretching is a great way to warm up for a workout and cool down after exercise. But does it work as well as yoga?

The answer depends on what you're looking for.

Yoga is more than just stretching. It's an ancient practice that also includes deep breathing, meditation, and relaxation techniques as its main focus. In short, yoga has a lot to offer – but it may not be the best choice if you want to focus primarily on stretching.

Yoga also takes time to learn. You'll need several months before you're ready to perform many of the poses that are part of yoga practice. Some people, however, believe that yoga is superior to other forms of exercise because it uses both active and passive forms of stretching. You might want to try a beginner class first or ask your doctor whether he or she thinks yoga would be good for you.

The bottom line? Both yoga and stretching are good options for improving flexibility and reducing muscle soreness of the muscles and joints; however, if you're interested in improving your athletic performance or preventing injury during a strength-training workout, stretching may be your best bet!

Stretching each part of your body

Did you know that most people spend at least a third of their day with their necks flexed forward? This postural habit leads to chronic neck pain and contributes to decreased mobility. Neck stretching can help improve your posture and reduce tension in your shoulders, neck, and upper back.

As you age, the muscles in your neck tend to lose their flexibility. This makes it harder to maintain good posture, leading to neck and upper back pain. Neck stretching is often recommended as part of a home exercise program for people who have chronic neck pain or stiffness. These stretches can be done while sitting or while standing up. In some cases, you may need to use a towel or pillow to help keep your head in place during the stretch.

The neck muscles are attached to the head at the base of the skull, and they control the movement of the head. There are seven different types of neck muscles, but not all of them are involved in all movements. When you stretch your neck, you're trying to increase how far you can move your head in each direction. Doing this increases your neck's overall flexibility - which is always a good thing!

Neck stretches can be done any time during the day when you feel like it - perhaps just before getting out of bed or after sitting on your couch for too long. Neck stretching is one of the best ways to maintain good spinal health because it helps counteract all the time we spend hunched over in front of the tv or smartphones.

When you think about it, you use your neck almost every time you move or turn your head. As a result, your neck muscles are constantly working to support you. The strain they endure can lead to problems like tension, headaches, and muscle spasms.

Stretching can help relieve these symptoms and keep your neck healthy. But when is the ideal time to stretch it? Here are some times when it makes sense to take a few minutes to stretch your neck:

Before bed. Stretching before going to sleep will help relax your neck muscles, reducing pain and improving your ability to fall asleep.

After waking up. Stretching the neck after you wake up helps counteract the effects of sleeping with your head in a flexed position all night long.

After sitting down or engaging in an activity for too long. If you spend most of the day sitting, gardening, or cleaning, it's important to take breaks from what you're doing and stretch the neck for about 2-3 minutes each time.

For chronic headaches, stretching helps relieve muscle tension in the neck and upper back muscles. It also reduces pressure on nerves that may be causing pain. Stretching the neck is also recommended for people with arthritis and other conditions that cause joint stiffness and immobility of the neck joints.

The rule of thumb is that you should never stretch your neck or any joint right after you've injured it. For example, if you whiplash your neck in an accident, you shouldn't try to stretch it until the pain goes away.

The shoulder, on the other hand, is a ball-and-socket joint, and it's one of the most mobile joints in the body. This means that it can move in almost any direction – up and down, side to side, front to back.

But that mobility comes at a cost: The shoulder joint is also made of some of the least durable tissues in your body. If you spend too much time sitting with your shoulders rounded forward, or if you practice yoga poses that force you into extreme ranges of motion, you'll likely experience pain in the front of your shoulder.

The shoulder is made up of three joints: the glenohumeral joint (where your upper arm meets your shoulder), acromioclavicular joint (where your collarbone meets your shoulder), and sternoclavicular joint (where your collarbone meets your sternum).

When these joints become stiff or immobile, they can cause discomfort in the muscles surrounding them. The rotator cuff muscles are particularly vulnerable to this type of injury because they cross two joints.

That's where shoulder stretching comes in. Stretching helps decrease muscle tension around the joint and improves mobility. It also decreases stress on tendons and ligaments and improves blood circulation throughout the area.

Stretching isn't just for athletes or yoga devotees; it's an important part of any fitness routine for anyone who wants to prevent injury or maintain flexibility over time. Shoulder stretching is a great way to relieve tension, improve posture, and reduce shoulder pain.

Stretching can help ease the pain that comes with bad posture, which is especially common among those who had a desk job in the past. When you're seated all day, your muscles become stiff and tight, leading to back pain and even joint problems. Shoulder stretches can also help you achieve better posture. By strengthening your upper body, you'll be able to hold yourself up straight for long periods.

When muscles are tense, they restrict blood flow and prevent nutrients from getting through – this makes them feel sore and tight. Stretching shoulders increases blood flow in the area by opening up the muscle tissue so more oxygen-rich blood can flow through it. This improves circulation throughout the shoulders, giving you more energy and relieving muscle fatigue.

These stretches also benefit people who suffer from shoulder injuries and those who want to prevent injuries. You can also use stretches to relieve stress and ease chronic shoulder pain.

The best time to stretch the shoulders is after a workout or any physical activity that causes muscle soreness. This is because stretching helps loosen up the muscles that have been working hard and may be tight or stiff.

Simply standing up and reaching your arms behind you can be enough to loosen up tight muscles in the back of the shoulder blade. If this doesn't work, try lying on a yoga mat, placing a pillow under your head, and stretching out your arms with palms facing down toward the floor.

But shoulders aren't as near as problematic as back pain for older adults. In fact, back pain is the second most common reason people go to the doctor, and it's the leading cause of disability worldwide. It can be caused by injury or trauma, but in most cases, it's due to overuse and muscle overstretching.

Back pain may also be caused by poor posture or muscle imbalances. Our bodies can handle this type of abuse when we're young because we have plenty of time to recover from injuries and build muscle strength. But as we get older, back pain becomes more common and more difficult to treat.

Stretching doesn't just benefit your physical health – it can also help improve your mental health by reducing stress levels and improving your mood. Stretching your back can help alleviate back pain, improve posture, and increase flexibility.

When you strengthen your back muscles, you are making them shorter. To maintain a balance between the strength and flexibility of your back muscles, it's important to stretch them regularly.

Stretching your back helps to keep your spine flexible and free of stiffness. Sitting for long periods without stretching out your back muscles may become tight and stiff. This can lead to pain in the lower back area when standing or walking around.

Regular back stretching will also help with spinal posture by improving muscle tone throughout the body and increasing flexibility in the spine and surrounding muscles. Stretching your back will also help improve circulation, which reduces swelling in the lower back area. This may cause pain or stiffness in the low back region when standing up straight or walking around after sitting down for a long period.

You should stretch your back whenever it feels tight or sore. But there are also some specific times when stretching is especially beneficial. The answer depends on your goals. Try basic stretches if you're trying to loosen up stiff muscles before exercise. This is an ideal way to prepare your body for any activity that involves bending over, such as gardening or golfing.

If your goal is to improve flexibility and prevent injury, try a more advanced stretch like the cobra pose. This pose helps to lengthen tight muscles in the upper back and shoulders while strengthening muscles in your lower back. For many people, stretching the back is a great way to relax after work or exercise. It can help relieve tension in the back and shoulders caused by sitting all day or carrying heavy objects around.

Stretching may not help with acute pain, but it can relieve chronic pain caused by conditions such as arthritis or spinal stenosis. Stretching exercises seem helpful for people with chronic lower-back pain," says Timothy Griffin, MD, Associate Professor of Physical Medicine and Rehabilitation at Duke University Medical Center in Durham, NC. These exercises also help improve strength and balance while reducing joint stress.

One of the most neglected areas of the bodies older adults fail to stretch: the legs. The main reason for leg stretching is to improve the mobility of your legs. This is important because when you have stiff muscles, it can lead to back pain and other problems. By increasing the flexibility of your lower body, you can reduce issues in other areas of your body and increase your comfort.

Leg stretching can also help with muscle soreness after exercise or other activities by increasing blood flow to the area. This helps flush out excess lactic acid that builds up during exercise, reducing soreness and speeding up recovery time after exercise. Finally, leg stretching will also improve strength in your lower body by helping build muscle mass in these areas.

When you stretch your legs, you increase the range of motion of your knees, ankles, and hips. This improves coordination and balance, which are important for injury prevention. Leg stretches also improve circulation to your lower extremities, which can help prevent swelling in your feet and legs.

If you are a beginner at stretching, it is important to know when to stretch your legs and when not to. Seniors should stretch their legs twice daily, once in the morning and once before bedtime. However, if you feel like doing so during the day, then go ahead.

Stretching should be part of your routine if you are more active or simply like exercising. You may start slow with some basic stretches at first. Still, as you get more comfortable with it, you can increase the intensity of your stretching and the number of repetitions you do each time.

To keep your body healthy and functioning, you must find ways to train your muscles. A good place to start is with some light stretching. Don't worry - you won't ever have to overdo it or get tired. Continue reading the next chapters and just follow along!

Chapter 2: Morning Stretches

When you wake up, you're entering a new day. Your body and mind are at their peak performance. Waking up is a complex process involving many different brain parts. It begins with the eyes, which signal the brain that it's time to wake up. The brain then sends signals back to the muscles and organs to prepare for wakefulness.

The most obvious sign of waking up is when you open your eyes. But even before that, there are signs that you're starting to come around: blinking, twitching, and rolling over in bed.

Once your eyes are open, you'll start to notice other muscle movements as part of the "pre-wake" stage of your morning routine – this prepares you for getting out of bed, using the bathroom, brushing your teeth, and so on.

These movements are controlled by a reticular formation (RF) part of your brain. The RF is responsible for keeping you asleep if there's no reason for you to be awake. If something happens that requires your attention – say, an alarm goes off – then the RF will send signals to another part of your brain called the thalamus, which wakes up other parts of your nervous system so that they can respond appropriately.

When you wake up, your temperature also increases. Your brain triggers a process called thermogenesis that raises your internal temperature again. This is why it feels so warm in your bed right before you get out of it.

Your blood pressure rises slightly upon awakening from sleep, then falls down within about 10 minutes after waking up for good. This is because the parasympathetic nervous system takes over once again and starts to calm things down after being inactive during deep sleep stages.

Your heart rate also speeds up. To meet the increased demand for oxygen, blood vessels in your lungs dilate, and blood flow increases to bring more oxygen into your system. Your heartbeat speeds up so more blood can be pumped through these vessels. This extra blood flow accounts for why people often experience palpitations when they first wake up - or even during the middle of the night if they've been tossing and turning too much!

While your body fully adjusts for the day, a morning stretch is a great way to wake up the body properly. As you get older, your body becomes less flexible, and it's important to keep it limber. Stretching in the morning can make a big difference in how well you feel throughout the day, both mentally and physically.

"Stretching helps improve circulation and makes muscles more flexible," says exercise physiologist Michele Olson, Ph.D., author of The New Rules of Lifting for Women. "It also helps wake up your body and improves mood."

A morning stretch can help to improve your posture and reduce any muscle tension that may be present in your body throughout that particular day. This will help to reduce any back pain or stiffness that you may be experiencing. It also increases energy levels throughout the day by increasing blood flow through your body. This means that all areas of your body will receive more oxygen and nutrients, which helps to boost energy levels.

Sitting for long periods can cause stress on your muscles and joints, leading to aches and pains. Performing a morning stretch will help to relieve some of this tension so that it doesn't build up throughout the day. Stretching also increases the production of naturally occurring chemicals in the brain that produce feelings of pleasure because it causes mild discomfort that's followed by relief when you stretch further than usual - a phenomenon known as "the pain-pleasure principle."

It is recommended to stretch for 5 to 10 minutes a day. This can be done in the morning or at night, but some older adults find it more effective to do it in the morning. If you're not a morning person, it might be hard to get started with stretches and other forms of exercise as soon as you wake up. But it's worth a try - research shows that starting your day with physical activity can improve your mood, energy levels, and concentration.

Stretching immediately after waking up is not a good idea because you're likely to be stiff from being in one position all night long. Instead, wait until you've been awake for 10-20 minutes or so before stretching - this will give your body time to warm up after being inactive all night long.

Suppose you're having trouble getting started with stretching or another form of exercise in the morning. In that case, you can set the alarm 15-30 minutes before you normally wake up. Or set it on a weekend when you have time to spare so you won't feel rushed. A trick that always works is to get out of bed as soon as the alarm goes off and brush your teeth or make the bed before you begin stretching. Here are 5-morning stretches that can help you wake up, get energized, and be ready to start your day.

Cat-cow pose

This is a great way to wake up your body and mind. Start by getting on all fours with shoulders over wrists, knees over ankles, and hands directly under shoulders. Inhale as you lift your head, tailbone, and chest towards the ceiling while pulling your belly button in towards your spine.

Exhale as you roll your shoulders forward while gently arching your back and lowering your head between your arms until it touches the floor or mat (not recommended if you have any neck issues). Repeat this 5-10 times until you feel more alert and energized!

Downward dog

Remain on all fours, just like on the cat-cow pose. With an inhale, lift your knees off the floor and straighten your legs as much as possible while keeping them parallel to one another (your heels may or may not touch the ground). With an exhale, flex at your elbows and push back into a downward dog position (hands flat on the floor with wrists aligned directly under shoulders). Keep pressing firmly into all four corners of each hand as you extend through the crown of the head.

Neck stretch

A neck stretch can be performed in the morning to help improve circulation, relieve muscle tension and prevent injury. The following neck stretches can be used to release tightness in the neck muscles and increase flexibility.

Neck flexion: Sit or stand up straight with your head level looking straight ahead. Slowly lean your head forward until you feel a gentle stretch in the back of your neck. Hold for 10 seconds, then repeat five times.

Neck extension: Sit or stand up straight with your head looking straight ahead. Slowly tilt your head back until you feel a gentle stretch in the front of your neck. Hold for 10 seconds, then repeat five times.

Chest stretch

Chest stretches are a great way to loosen up the chest and upper back muscles. The chest is made up of two different muscle groups: the pectoralis major and the pectoralis minor. The pectoralis major covers much of the upper chest, while the pectoralis minor is located underneath it. Stretching these muscles helps to improve flexibility in your shoulders, which can lead to less injury over time.

Stand with your feet a few inches apart, toes facing forward. Inhale, place your arms behind your back, and slowly bend forward at the waist until you feel a gentle stretch in the front of your chest (you can also bend from side to side). Hold for 10 seconds or as long as you like, then return to the starting position and repeat several times on each side.

Shoulder rolls

Shoulder rolls are a great way to loosen up your upper body. They can be done in many different variations. The most basic shoulder roll involves simply rolling your shoulders forward and backward. You can also add some variety by doing shoulder rolls with your arms bent at the elbows, then straightened out so it resembles a wave motion.

A few simple stretches can help you feel more energized, less stressed, and just happier in general. Whether you're a morning person or not, stretching is one of the best ways to start your day. It gives you an immediate sense of calm and helps wake up your body and mind.

But did you know that stretching helps you with your mental health? Stretching helps improve mood and reduce stress levels. It helps relieve depression, anxiety, and fatigue because of how much oxygen it fills your body with. This leads to better oxygenation of the brain. A study published in The Journal of Sports Medicine & Physical Fitness found that regular stretching improved mental health by lowering anxiety levels by 18 percent compared to those who didn't stretch regularly.

Chapter 3: Evening Stretches

Your body is affected by what you do during the day, so if you sit all day, you will be less tired and might find it harder to fall asleep. If you are active during the day, you will feel more relaxed by the evening.

As the sun sets, your body begins to change. Blood pressure lowers, heart rate slows down, and digestion stops. The muscles relax, and the brain releases hormones that make you sleepy.

You may notice that your breathing becomes deeper and slower as your body prepares for sleep. The parasympathetic nervous system turns on and slows down the central nervous system so it can rest. The adrenal glands release stress hormones into the bloodstream to help you calm down before bedtime.

In the evening, the body goes into repair mode. The immune system starts rebuilding after fighting off infections and diseases after one day. Blood flow increases in the skin, which helps remove toxins from our cells. Tissues throughout our bodies are repaired as well – including muscles that might have been damaged during exercise or movement during the day.

During the evening, our bodies also get warmer because we move around and generate heat through exercise or activity. But as soon as we stop moving around, our temperature drops – especially if we're inside an air-conditioned building like a mall or movie theater.

When that happens, we start feeling tired because we're not generating enough heat to keep ourselves warm. The body temperature typically drops about 1 degree Fahrenheit per hour after sunset, meaning if it was 100 degrees at noon, it would be 99 degrees at 7 p.m., 98 degrees at 8 p.m., and 97 degrees by 9 p.m.

A great time to stretch is right before bedtime. Studies have found that doing so improves sleep quality by reducing stress and anxiety levels, which can interfere with restful sleep. Stretching relieves stress, improves sleep quality, and reduces anxiety. It can also help you unwind after a long day and prepare your body for bedtime.

Stretching has also been shown to help people fall asleep faster and stay asleep longer. This is especially beneficial for people who have trouble falling asleep or staying asleep at night. If you have trouble with insomnia, stretching is a simple way to boost your sleep quality without making any major changes in your life or disrupting your schedule.

A study published in The Journal of Sports Medicine found that pre-bedtime stretching significantly improved sleep quality in people who had trouble falling asleep at night. The stretches used in this study were designed specifically for athletes, but any type of stretch will help improve your sleep quality if performed before bedtime.

Nighttime stretching increases blood flow throughout the body—including to areas like your hips and ankles that might not get enough oxygen when sitting all day long or watching TV at home. This helps reduce stiffness and soreness in those areas, so you feel better throughout the day (and night!).

Stretching before bed can also help prevent muscle soreness in the morning. The problem is that most people don't stretch enough during the day, so they're more likely to experience soreness. Stretching before bed helps to keep muscles loose and flexible throughout the night, so they're less likely to tighten up while you sleep and become sore when you wake up.

If you don't stretch regularly, you may find yourself waking up with stiff muscles or sore joints. These problems can be especially troublesome if they happen in the middle of the night while you're trying to get back to sleep after waking up briefly or tossing and turning for hours.

It also might improve your physical health. It's linked to lower blood pressure, reduced risk of heart disease and stroke, and a reduced risk of type 2 diabetes. The reason for this is unclear, but one theory suggests that stretching may increase blood flow through arteries and veins, which helps reduce blood pressure over time.

Nighttime anxiety is the world's most common mental health issue, affecting around 40 million adults in the United States alone. It's also one of the most common reasons people visit their primary care doctors, who can prescribe medication to help manage symptoms.

But there are other ways to cope with anxiety as well. Stretching has been shown to reduce stress and anxiety levels. This may be because exercise helps improve sleep quality, which in turn reduces stress and improves mood.

If you're looking for an effective way to relax at night before bedtime, try stretching before you go to sleep instead of reaching for your phone or TV remote control.

A study published in the Journal of Bodywork and Movement Therapies found that nighttime stretching can reduce anxiety levels. The researchers discovered that stretching reduces anxiety by increasing serotonin levels in the brain, which is important for feelings of calmness, happiness, and relaxation.

Serotonin is also known as the "happy chemical" because it contributes to positive moods and feelings of overall well-being. It's no surprise that serotonin is one of the key ingredients in antidepressants like Prozac and Zoloft!

To relieve anxiety, start your stretch routine by practicing deep breathing. Breathing is the most fundamental of all the body's physiological functions. As we breathe, air enters and leaves the lungs, providing us with oxygen and removing carbon dioxide. The respiratory center in the brainstem controls our breathing rate and depth.

During stress, breathing becomes rapid and shallow. This results from an increased sympathetic nervous system activity that triggers faster breathing – a protective response to prepare the body for action (fight or flight). This pattern can become habitual when an individual experiences chronic stress.

The practice of deep breathing has been used for centuries to reduce anxiety by controlling rapid breathing patterns. Deep breathing helps us slow down our respiration rate to calm down and relax our bodies and minds.

To practice deep breathing, find a quiet place where you will not be disturbed. Then sit comfortably with your spine straight but relaxed and your shoulders relaxed as well (not hunched forward). Close your eyes or focus on a point in front of you so that all other distractions are eliminated from your mind.

Then focus on your breathing. Breathe in through your nose for five seconds, hold it for two seconds, then exhale slowly through pursed lips for six seconds (or until it feels like the air has left your body). Repeat this cycle four times (five breaths total). Pay attention to how it feels. Feel the air going into your nose as it passes through your nostrils and then fills up your lungs with oxygen from deep inside your body. This will help bring more oxygen into your body, which will help calm you down even more! Combining deep breathing with nighttime stretches can get even better results.

Here are some stretches you can do that will help you better fall asleep:

Back Stretch

A back stretch gets rid of muscle tension in the upper body. Before starting any back stretch, make sure you are free of any injuries or health issues with your back. The back stretch loosens up tight muscles. It also helps to improve posture and relieve stress.

To do this stretch, stand with your feet about 3-4 feet apart. Bend forward at your waist until your upper body is parallel to the floor. Keep your head up and look forward as you bend over with your hands stretched behind you. Hold the position for 10-30 seconds, then straighten up slowly. Repeat the exercise 5 times for each leg.

This exercise is especially good for people who spend a lot of time sitting or standing in one place. If you spend most of your time at a desk or driving in a car, give yourself an extra few minutes before bed to do this simple exercise. You'll feel much better afterward!

Hamstring Stretch

The hamstring stretch is a simple exercise that can be done before you fall asleep. It improves flexibility and helps prevent injury. The hamstring stretch is probably the most well-known of all stretches and is used to relieve tightness in the back of the leg. The muscle group being stretched is called your hamstrings, which are three muscles on the back of your upper leg.

Lie on your back with your feet flat on the floor and your knees straight. Raise one knee upward while keeping the other foot slightly elevated from the floor. Pull gently on your bent leg until you start feeling it in your thigh. Hold for 15 to 20 seconds before switching sides.

Side Stretch

The side stretch is an easy way to stretch the muscle group that runs from your spine to your core. This muscle group helps support the spine, so it's important to keep it flexible.

Stand with your feet wide apart. Bend sideways and stretch your hand to the direction you are stretching your core. Exhale as you slowly lower yourself until you feel a gentle pull in your low back and abdominal area. Hold this position for 10 to 30 seconds before slowly returning to a starting position by straightening up again while breathing in through your nose and out through pursed lips as you do so.

Pelvic tilt

The Pelvic Tilt Stretch is a great way to stretch your lower back and hip flexors. You'll also be working on your posture by keeping your chest up.

To do this exercise, you simply need a flat surface (you can use the edge of a bench or a table). Put one foot on the ground and your hands on the bench/table. Then lean forward until you feel a stretch in your glutes and hamstrings. Hold this position for 10 seconds, then come back up.

Repeat this 5 times on each side. If you want to make the stretch more intense, you can lean forward with more weight on your hands and feet, but it's recommended to stay with just body weight for now so that you don't risk hurting yourself!

The Child's Pose

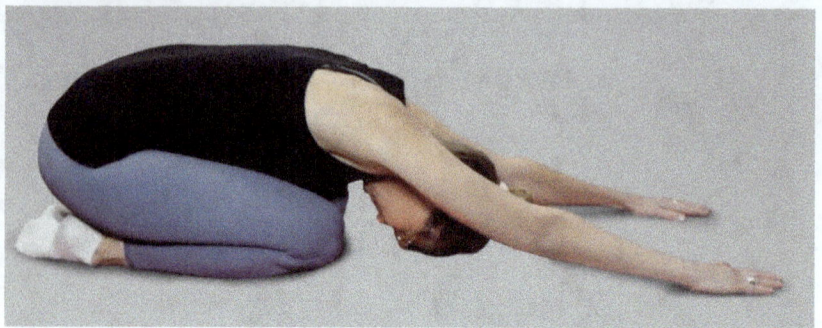

The Child's Pose relieves back pain, stretches your hips and shoulders, and calms your mind. The Child's Pose stretches the thighs, groin, shoulders and chest, spine, neck, hips, and ankles. It can help release tension in these areas by gently stretching the body.

Sit on the floor with your legs straight out in front of you. Bend your knees if it makes it more comfortable for you. Place your hands on the floor behind you with palms flat on the ground. Press down into your hands and lift your buttocks off the floor so that only your feet are touching it – this will give your upper body support from below as well as above (if you don't have much flexibility in your hamstrings).

With knees bent or straight out in front of you, lower yourself down onto all fours and rest on your forearms or elbows. If kneeling is too uncomfortable, try sitting on heels or leaning against a wall instead.

Researchers at the University of California, Berkeley, found that stretching before bedtime helped improve people's moods and reduced their anxiety levels. The study involved 33 people divided into two groups: one group did a 15-minute stretching routine before bed, while the other group did nothing. Both groups were then asked to complete surveys about how they were feeling and give saliva samples so that researchers could measure their stress levels.

After seven days, those who had practiced yoga had lower levels of cortisol – a hormone linked to stress – as well as less depression and anxiety than those who didn't do anything beforehand.

Chapter 4: Core Exercises & Stretching

Regular exercise has also been shown to reduce depression symptoms in seniors. It may help prevent dementia in older adults with mild cognitive impairment (MCI). Studies show that physically active adults have a lower risk of developing Alzheimer's disease and other forms of dementia later in life. Experts believe physical activity may protect the brain by improving blood flow or stimulating new neural connections between neurons in the brain's memory center (hippocampus).

The benefits of exercise are numerous, and they're even greater if you're 60 or older. Regular physical activity can improve your health and quality of life, reduce the risk of many chronic diseases and help you maintain independence.

"Exercise is one of the most powerful tools we have to promote health and wellness," says Scott Rodeo, MD, clinical professor of medicine at Stanford University School of Medicine in California. "And there's no better time than now to get started."

In addition to helping you maintain a healthy weight and prevent coronary artery disease (CAD), exercising for seniors also helps improve mental health, sleep quality, balance, and strength – all important factors in preventing falls. Here are some benefits core exercises and stretching help you with:

Improves Bone Health

As we age, our bodies also begin to lose bone density, and this bone loss makes us more prone to fractures if we fall. For this reason, seniors need to strengthen their bones because it helps them from becoming too fragile. This can lead to osteoporosis, a condition in which bones become weak and brittle.

The skeleton's main function is to support the body, protect internal organs and provide an attachment for muscles. Bones are made of cells called osteoblasts and osteoclasts that work together to create a network of proteins. In addition, bones are made up of blood vessels and nerves that allow them to function properly.

Osteoporosis occurs when there is a loss of calcium from the bones, causing them to become brittle and break easily. As the body ages, it loses bone mass faster than it can be replaced by new bone tissue – this leads to weakened bones that are more susceptible to fractures. It's important to note that while people with osteoporosis may suffer from fractures due to weakened bones, they may not have any symptoms at all until they've already suffered one or more fractures.

Exercise can improve bone health by increasing bone density and strength. It also builds muscle mass, which helps support healthy bones. When you exercise, your muscles contract and relax, and it's this contraction and relaxation that builds bone density.

Exercise also increases blood flow to the bones, which helps deliver which helps remove waste products from the body. This keeps the bones healthy and strong. It can also help reduce the risk of osteoporosis by preventing bone loss as people age. It does this by increasing muscle mass, which helps offset bone loss due to aging processes such as decreased hormone levels or menopause.

The American College of Sports Medicine recommends adults ages 65 and older should get at least 2 hours and 30 minutes per week of moderate-intensity aerobic activity or 1 hour and 15 minutes per week of vigorous aerobic activity – such as brisk walking or jogging – plus two days per week of strength training that works all major muscle groups (legs, hips, back, abdomen).

If you're older than 65 or have been diagnosed with osteoporosis or low bone density, talk to your doctor before starting an exercise program. Your doctor can tell you if any exercises are right for you based on your current health status.

Improves cardiovascular strength

Exercise improves cardiovascular strength by increasing heart rate and blood pressure, which improves oxygen flow throughout the body. This is especially important for people with heart disease, who have less oxygen-rich blood, to begin with.

Exercise also reduces inflammation and stress hormones, which can damage blood vessels, says Dr. Stanley Goldfarb, a professor of medicine at the University of Pennsylvania School of Medicine. Exercise helps people maintain a healthy weight and lower their risk for diabetes and high cholesterol – both of which are risk factors for heart disease.

In addition to improving cardiovascular strength, exercise increases lung capacity and muscle mass, which improves breathing and reduces fatigue during physical activity. One study found that people who exercised for at least 150 minutes each week had a lower risk of dying from all causes than those who didn't exercise or only did a light activity like walking or gardening. Another study followed 28,000 men for 14 years and found that those who did moderate-intensity exercise were less likely to die from any cause than men who didn't exercise.

Reduce the risk of dementia

Exercise is one of the best ways to keep your brain healthy. It can improve memory, reduce stress, and slow down the onset of dementia and depression. It's also a great way to keep your brain active and make learning new things easier.

Research has shown that physical activity helps protect against dementia by increasing blood flow to the brain, reducing inflammation, and improving insulin sensitivity. Exercise also boosts the production of nerve-protecting proteins in the brain.

People who exercise regularly are less likely than others to develop early signs of cognitive decline, such as memory problems or poor reasoning ability. And even if people already have mild cognitive impairment (MCI), which is an early stage of dementia, regular physical activity could prevent it from progressing into full-blown Alzheimer's disease (AD) or other dementias.

Studies suggest that people who do aerobic exercise — such as walking briskly on a treadmill — have a lower risk of developing AD than those who don't exercise or engage in an aerobic activity regularly enough. However, it's not clear whether this is because aerobic exercise reduces the risk of AD or because it keeps people healthier overall. They're less likely to develop other health problems that lead to dementia.

Another study published in January 2017 found that people who exercised regularly had a lower risk of developing mild cognitive impairment. The study followed 1,237 people aged 70 or older for an average of 4 years. Those who reported exercising regularly had a 39% lower risk of MCI than those who did not exercise.

Prevents falls

Falls are the leading cause of injury-related death and hospitalization in America. In addition, falls are associated with an increased risk of loss of mobility, depression, and other adverse health outcomes. The risk of falls is a major concern for older adults, but it's something you can work to minimize.

According to the Centers for Disease Control, falls are a leading cause of injury deaths among older adults. The CDC found that one in three adults 65 and older falls annually, and one in five causes moderate-to-severe injuries.

Exercise is one way that seniors can help prevent falls. The National Council on Aging (NCOA) recommends that seniors get at least 30 minutes of physical activity five days per week to reduce the risk of falling. The NCOA also suggests taking part in activities such as walking or dancing that require balance and coordination skills.

The good news is that even small amounts of exercise can boost your overall health and help reduce the risk of falls. If you haven't exercised in a while, start slowly with walking or other light aerobic activities. Then gradually increase the intensity of your workouts so that you can gain the greatest benefits from exercise.

When people think about fall prevention, they often focus on medications and other medical interventions that can help reduce their risk of falling. But exercise is an important part of fall prevention too. And when done properly, exercise can be just as effective as medication in preventing falls among older adults who are at high risk for falling or who have already fallen once or twice before.

In a study published in the Journal of Bone and Joint Surgery, researchers found that people who exercised at least twice a week had a lower risk of falling than those who exercised less frequently or not at all. If you already have osteoarthritis or have been diagnosed with osteoporosis, this study may not apply to you because exercise can increase your risk of falling.

If you fall once or twice, it does not necessarily cause concern – but if it happens frequently or if the falls result in injury (such as broken bones), then seeing a doctor is important to determine the cause and how to prevent future falls.

Better Quality Sleep

Exercise is a great way for seniors to combat sleep problems. Exercise can help seniors fall asleep more easily, stay asleep longer and get more restful sleep. The benefits of exercise are well known and proven. However, it's not only the physical benefits that matter but also the mental ones.

In addition to calming your mind and body, exercise also increases the brain's endorphins (feel-good hormones). Researchers from the University of Oklahoma Health Sciences Center examined how exercise affects sleep quality, sleepiness, and fatigue among sedentary adults. They found that regular physical activity improved sleep quality and reduced insomnia symptoms.

"Our findings highlight the importance of regular aerobic exercise as a means to promote healthy sleep patterns," said lead author Elizabeth Loder, Ph.D., associate professor of neurology at Harvard Medical School. "Based on this research, sedentary adults looking for ways to improve their sleep may want to consider adopting a regular exercise routine."

For this study, researchers recruited 72 sedentary adults between 18 and 65 who reported having difficulty falling asleep or staying asleep at least once per week in the past month. Participants were randomly assigned to either an exercise group or a control group that did not participate in any intervention during the nine weeks of study participation. The exercise group participated in three supervised exercise sessions per week for nine weeks, while the control group did not participate in any intervention during this period. The ones who added an exercise routine fell asleep faster and had lower anxiety levels than the control group.

Builds muscle mass

As we age, our muscles begin to lose mass. This loss of muscle mass is called sarcopenia and can be accelerated by chronic illness, immobility, and decreased physical activity. Sarcopenia is a serious problem for seniors because it leads to weakness, falls, and fractures, resulting in hospitalization or death.

Sarcopenia is often called "age-related atrophy" because it affects all muscles, from those in the arms and legs to those in the heart and lungs. As we get older, our bodies don't rebuild muscle tissue as well as they used to. The average person loses between 5% and 10% of their lean muscle tissue every decade after age 40. This can cause a decrease in strength and mobility over time.

The good news is that you can slow down the effects of sarcopenia by staying active, eating right, and getting enough sleep. Sarcopenia differs from other types of age-related muscle loss because it occurs independently from other comorbidities such as osteoporosis or obesity.

The prevalence of sarcopenia is estimated at 30% among community-dwelling elderly individuals. Sarcopenia has been associated with poor health outcomes, including increased mortality and morbidity, reduced quality of life, and functional independence. In addition to age-related factors, other factors can contribute to sarcopenia, including the following:

Inactivity: A lack of exercise can lead to a loss of muscle mass and strength over time.

Medications: Some medications, such as steroids, can cause weight gain in some people, which increases the risk of sarcopenia due to excess pounds being carried by the skeletal muscles instead of fat tissue. Other medications, such as statins, may reduce cholesterol levels too low and cause side effects such as weakness or fatigue, resulting in decreased mobility and difficulty performing tasks that require physical effort, like cooking or cleaning around the house.

Dietary habits: Poor eating habits can affect your metabolism and increase body fat while simultaneously decreasing lean body mass (muscle), which contributes to the development of sarcopenia.

Muscle is built through a process called hypertrophy, which means "enlargement." You can find hypertrophy examples around you in nature – think of a tree trunk that grows the more the plant gets fed or a balloon that expands when blown up. The muscles in your body are made up of long strands of protein called actin and myosin. These proteins work together to pull on each other and create movement. When you exercise, these strands break down, causing the muscles to grow larger over time.

The main way that muscle gets bigger is by adding more protein to it. This happens during the recovery period after exercise when your body is repairing damaged tissue and making new muscle fibers stronger than before.

To get bigger muscles from exercise, you need to exercise enough to cause damage to your muscles. This damage triggers an inflammatory response in which your body repairs the damage by making new fibers stronger than before.

Our muscles are made up of protein, and protein is made up of amino acids. When we exercise, our muscles begin to break down their proteins to build new muscle tissue (and repair damaged muscle). The amino acids from the broken down proteins are recycled through the bloodstream to make new muscle proteins.

Our bodies rely on our tissues for amino acid recycling during exercise to compensate for the shortfall in dietary protein. As we exercise, our bodies release hormones such as cortisol and adrenaline into our bloodstream. These hormones stimulate our bodies to release more insulin than usual to absorb more sugar from our bloodstreams into our cells (to fuel energy production).

When we have more insulin in our bloodstream than normal, it causes a shift in amino acid transport through cell membranes. Amino acids move out of cells and into blood vessels more easily than normal when insulin levels are high because fewer transport proteins are available on cell membranes.

Exercising your core is not just for fitness fanatics and bodybuilders. They can be extremely helpful for everyone, from the elderly to the very young, in reducing the risk of injury and improving overall health. Core exercises involve a lot of muscle groups and help strengthen your body from head to toe. Core exercises are one of the most important elements of any fitness program.

A core exercise is any type of exercise that focuses on strengthening the muscles in your midsection. These muscles include those in your abdomen, lower back, hip flexors, hamstrings, and glutes. A strong core helps prevent injury by allowing you to maintain good posture while performing other activities such as walking or gardening.

It also helps protect your spine by providing support throughout most daily movements, such as bending over or lifting objects off the ground. A strong core will also improve balance, which is essential for preventing falls among older adults. Strengthening your core is an important part of maintaining a healthy lifestyle. It can help you maintain a healthy weight, improve your mood and energy levels, reduce stress, boost your immune system and prevent disease.

If you're over 65, this exercise can also help you manage chronic conditions like arthritis and diabetes. And it's never too late to start exercising – even if you've been sedentary all your life! Exercise helps keep your metabolism working at its peak, which can help you maintain a healthy weight throughout life. It also helps you build muscle tissue, which increases your metabolic rate even more. And because muscle tissue burns more calories than fat tissue, your body uses more fat as fuel when it has more muscle tissue.

Here are some exercises and stretches to strengthen your core:

Wall stretch

The wall stretch is an easy way to work your entire abdominal wall, as well as your lower back muscles. This is a good stretch to do before or after a workout because it increases flexibility without putting any pressure on the spine.

Stand with your back against a wall, feet hip-width apart, and arms at your sides. Bend your knees until you feel a stretch in your hamstring muscles (the backs of your thighs). Hold for 30 seconds or until you feel the tension ease out of your hamstrings. You should not feel any tightness in your lower back or abs during this stretch. Repeat 3 times on each side.

Plank

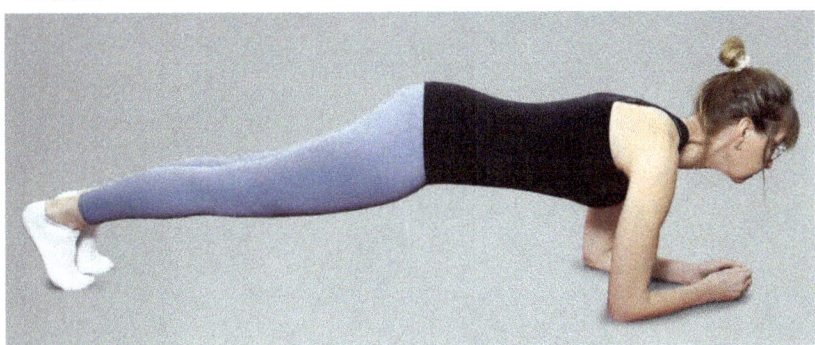

The plank is a great exercise for seniors because it works several muscles at once. The plank works your core, lower back, glutes, hamstrings, and shoulders. The best way to do this exercise is to get into a push-up position with your elbows on the floor and hands directly under your shoulders.

Then slowly lower yourself so that you're resting on your forearms. Hold this position for as long as possible – take deep breaths while you're holding it. You'll feel a burn in your abs, glutes, and back muscles when you hold this pose for longer than 10 seconds. If you find it hard to achieve, you can do the plank with your knees on the floor.

Reverse crunch

This exercise targets your lower abs, which will help create a flatter stomach and stronger core muscles in general. To do this exercise: Lie on your back with knees bent toward your chest; place hands behind your head or by hips (whichever feels most comfortable).

Lift feet off the ground while keeping legs together; raise hips off the ground until they form a straight line with the body (don't let knees bend past toes). Lower back down slowly until just before the bottoms of feet touch the ground - don't let them touch yet!

Squats

Squats work your legs and lower back muscles while strengthening your core muscles at the same time. You can do squats by holding onto a chair or countertop for balance if necessary. If you want to increase the intensity of this exercise, hold weights in each hand or wear ankle weights around your ankles while doing squats as well as during other exercises that require lifting objects off the floor (such as lifting groceries).

Bird Dog Exercise

Bird Dogs are a great exercise to get your back and core muscles in shape. This is a great exercise to help you improve your balance and coordination as well. The bird dog is often used as part of rehabilitation programs for people who have suffered from an injury, but it can also be used by anyone interested in improving their overall health and fitness.

Start by lying on all fours. Then lift one leg up at a time so that both legs are straight with toes pointed out. Now lift the opposite arm up at the same time so that you are balancing on one arm and one leg at a time. Repeat this exercise as many times as possible before resting again.

Sit-ups

Sit-ups are one of the most well-known core exercises. To perform a sit-up, lie on your back with your knees bent and feet flat on the floor. Place your hands behind your head, fingers interlaced, and elbows out wide. Tighten your abdominal muscles and lift your torso until it's almost perpendicular to the floor. Slowly lower yourself back down until you're flat again. Repeat 5 times, working up to three sets.

Bicycle crunches

Bicycle crunches are another great way to strengthen your core muscles and their surrounding connective tissue; they also improve circulation throughout these areas and help prevent hemorrhoids by strengthening pelvic muscles that support veins in this area.

To perform bicycle crunches, lie on your back with hands behind your head and legs extended straight out so they're parallel with the floor; keep your legs together throughout the exercise. Pull right knee toward chest while reaching left hand toward right knee; without resting lower leg back down to start position while returning hand behind. Repeat 6 times on each leg.

Chapter 5: Routines for Daily Activity

Stretching is essential for helping your body recover from any physical activity. When you perform any type of physical activity, including exercise or work around the house, your muscles contract to produce energy and move your body parts.

As soon as you stop exercising or working, your muscles relax again. However, if you don't stretch after physical activity, your muscles remain contracted until they naturally release on their own - which may take as long as 30 minutes!

Many people don't realize just how important stretching is to their health until they experience an injury that could have been prevented with regular stretching exercises. When people get injured, many times it's because they didn't warm up properly or didn't stretch afterward. To prevent injury from activities like gardening, cleaning - or even walking - it's important to always stretch your body first.

Gardening

A gardening session can be a great way to get some exercise and enjoy the outdoors. However, if you're not careful, you could end up with an injury from overdoing it. Not only that, but gardening is an activity that causes muscle aches and soreness due to the repetitive nature of the work. It has many benefits, and one of the best is that it can help reduce stress.

By getting your hands dirty and working in the garden, you are engaging in a form of active meditation. Studies have shown that people who garden have lower blood pressure and cholesterol levels than non-gardeners. Gardening also helps you connect with nature and improves your mood by increasing serotonin production.

When you garden, you use several different muscle groups simultaneously. When lifting heavy objects or walking long distances, your legs are working hard to keep your body upright and stable. The muscles in your back help support the weight of any objects being moved and stabilize your body when bending over or lifting something heavy.

Your arms carry buckets full of dirt or other materials to transport them from one place to another. When weeding in rows, you'll use your arms to pull weeds out by their roots and throw them into piles for disposal later on. If your muscles are aching, try these stretches to help relieve pain from gardening:

Sideway Chest Stretch

This stretch helps relieve pain in the back and shoulders by stretching tight chest muscles. Stand with feet shoulder-width apart, knees slightly bent, arms straight with palms facing sideways. Take a deep breath and gently stretch your right arm behind you until you feel a slight stretch in your chest muscles. Hold for five seconds, then slowly return to starting position before repeating on the other side. Repeat 3-4 times on each side.

Arm stretch

Stand with your feet together, arms by your sides, and palms facing inward. Raise your right arm up toward the ceiling and lean to the right until you feel a stretch in the back of your right shoulder. Hold for 20 seconds, then repeat on the other side.

Shoulder Stretch

The shoulders bear most of our body weight as we work in the garden, so it's important to maintain flexibility in these muscles, so they don't get too tight and cause pain later on down the road. To perform this exercise, stand with feet shoulder-width apart and arms hanging loosely at your sides. Cross your arms in front of you before stretching them behind your back. Do this a few times to feel the pull in your shoulders.

Shopping

When you go shopping, your muscles work hard. A trip to the supermarket can be considered a workout. Shopping carts can weigh up to 50 pounds, and they're not made for comfort. The handles are often above shoulder height, and they're not ergonomically designed. But shopping is also an opportunity to strengthen your muscles – if you're willing to make the effort.

If you've never had much reason to think about how hard it is to push a full cart around a store, consider this: A study published in 2008 found that people with spinal injuries who used wheelchairs routinely burned more than 500 calories per day just going about their daily lives – nearly half their total daily energy needs.

The biggest challenge when pushing a cart is keeping your back straight and shoulders relaxed so that you can use your leg muscles instead of your back muscles," says Daniel Wibbelsman, head of research at the Lewis Institute for Rehabilitation Medicine. When you go shopping, your muscles are put through a lot of strain. Your legs are required to carry the heavy load, and your arms are used to carry all the bags. This can cause your arms and legs to ache when you return home.

Shopping can also affect your posture because you may be forced to lean forward in order to bend down and pick up items that are on the lower shelves of stores or shops. If this happens regularly, then it could lead to back problems in later years.

When you go shopping, your calves and quads will be working hard, as will your gluteus maximus. That's because most of our movements are forward or backward, so your body is constantly working against gravity. In fact, if you're carrying a heavy bag, your shoulders will also work hard during the day.

You'll find that your hamstrings get stretched out pretty quickly if they're not used to carrying heavy loads around all day long! Your shoulders may start to ache after carrying too much weight too high on your body for too long, but this can easily be remedied by using a backpack with strong straps. Your back muscles are going to feel it as well - especially if you don't use proper posture while carrying items around in a shopping center or department store!

If you're suffering from back pain after shopping, you're not alone. It's estimated that 80 percent of people will experience back pain at some point in their lives. To help prevent this pain and stiffness, try these stretching exercises before heading out:

Back Stretch

Lie on your stomach and place your hands behind your head. Gently push your head away from the floor as far as possible while keeping your elbows straight. Hold this position for 15-20 seconds, then relax.

Hip Rotator Stretch

Stand with feet shoulder-width apart, bend over at the hips with arms hanging down, reaching for your toes or until you feel a stretch in the groin area of one leg. Hold this position for 15-20 seconds, then relax before repeating on the other leg.

Upper Back Stretch

Sit down straight, keep your legs straight forward and reach for your toes until you feel a stretch in the hamstring muscle on that side of your body; hold this position for 15-20 seconds, then relax before repeating it one more time.

Cleaning

Cleaning can be tough on the body. After all, a lot of cleaning is done on your hands and knees, which can be uncomfortable and painful if you're not used to it. But how does cleaning affect your muscles?

While many people are aware that cleaning can be hard on your back and knees, they may not realize how much it can affect other parts of the body. Cleaning strains your upper body significantly.

To avoid back pain while doing chores around your home, make sure that you have good posture when bending over or crawling along the floor. For example, if you're mopping up spills or scrubbing floors, bend from the hips instead of leaning forward at the waist. This will help keep stress off of your lower back as well as prevent any unnecessary pain from occurring during your cleaning session.

Cleaning also requires a lot of arm work, especially when it comes to vacuuming or dusting surfaces around your home. This can cause strain in both arms as well as in the shoulders if you're reaching above shoulder height while cleaning. It also requires good balance skills because you're often balancing on one leg while reaching up high with the other leg – similar to what gymnasts do when they mount the balance beam or pommel horse.

A study in Japan found that housework burns an average of 100 calories per hour – not nearly as much as running at 6 mph or walking at 3 mph (about 225 calories per hour), but still enough to burn off about 2 1/2 pounds of fat over time if you clean every day.

The study suggests that cleaning is one of the most common causes of back pain. The weight of furniture, appliances, and other items can put a lot of strain on your back over time. When you lift heavy objects or bend over to pick up an object from the floor, you could injure yourself or cause an existing injury to worsen. Cleaning also puts a lot of pressure on the knees because they have to support your body weight while you're standing on them while doing various tasks around the house. This can lead to knee pain if done too often or without proper rest between sessions of cleaning.

If you have poor posture while cleaning, then this could lead to shoulder strain as well. You should always stand up straight when doing any task, whether it's cleaning or not! To ease muscle soreness after cleaning, try these stretches:

Shoulder stretch

Stand with your feet shoulder-width apart, keep a straight posture, and place your hands behind you while bending them 90 degrees. Gently press your elbows toward each other until you feel the muscles along both sides of your chest stretch. Hold for 10-20 seconds, and then switch sides. Repeat five times. This stretch helps relieve pain in the upper back and shoulders caused by hunching over, as well as helps improve posture by improving circulation and flexibility in those areas.

Bent-Knee Stretch

First, stand with your feet hip-width apart and your hands on your hips. Then bend forward until you feel a bit of tension in your hamstrings. Hold this position for 30 seconds, then repeat it two or three times.

Seated Forward Bend

This pose can be done while sitting on the floor or on a chair – either way, it helps improve spinal flexibility and circulation to reduce back pain and stiffness caused by bending over to clean floors. Start by folding forward at the waist until you feel a stretch along. Keep the position for 10-30 seconds and slowly get up into starting position.

Crossed leg stretch

The hip flexors attach to the front of your pelvis and allow you to lift your knee towards your chest. To stretch these muscles, lie on your back with one leg bent at a 90-degree angle, and the other crossed upon the bent legLift your straight leg off the floor as high as possible until you feel a stretch in your hip flexor. Hold this position for 10 seconds, then lower it back down slowly until it touches the floor again. Repeat this exercise 5 times.

Knitting/Sewing

Knitting is an easy way to keep your hands busy, and your mind focused. The repetitive motion of knitting can help you relax and manage stress. But you don't need to be a fitness expert to know that knitting makes muscles sore. The reason for this is that knitting puts a lot of stress on the muscles and joints, especially if you're new to it. If you've been knitting for a while, then your body will adapt, and you won't get sore as easily.

Most people experience soreness in their shoulders and arms after knitting for several hours at a time. The answer to why this happens lies in the mechanics of it. To knit, your fingers have to hold on to multiple strands at once and manipulate them through loops and around needles. Each time you do this, you're using a different set of muscles in your hands – which can make them feel sore afterward.

If you're new to knitting and would like to avoid the soreness, try taking frequent breaks from the activity (such as when watching TV). Also, make sure that you're using good posture while working with needles – sit up straight with your shoulders back, and elbows bent slightly away from your body.

When you knit, you stretch the fingers and wrists as you grab the needles and pull them through the stitches. This helps keep your hands flexible, so they don't become stiff with age. It also helps improve blood circulation, which can help with arthritis and carpal tunnel syndrome.

As you work on projects that require more complex stitches, like lace patterns or cables, your muscles will become stronger as they try to make sense of these patterns while moving the needles through the stitches. This strengthens muscles in your hands, arms, and shoulders – not just those used during knitting but also those used when lifting objects or carrying bags with both hands. Here are some hand stretches to help relieve tension in your hands, wrists, and arms:

Finger stretches

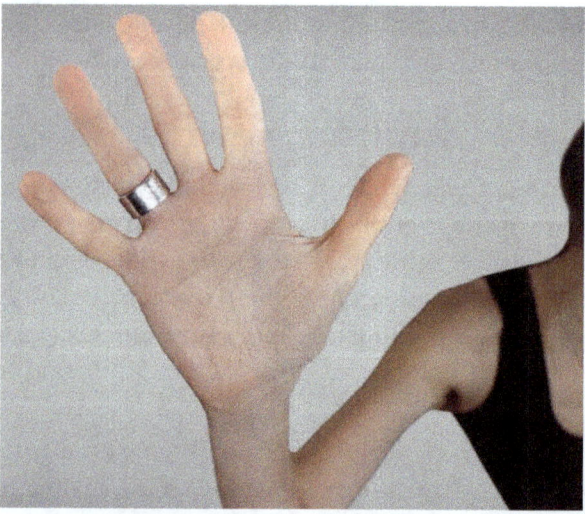

Spread fingers wide apart, hold for 10 seconds and relax. Repeat 5 times. This will help with pain in the thumb area due to gripping needles or yarn too tightly.

Palm stretches

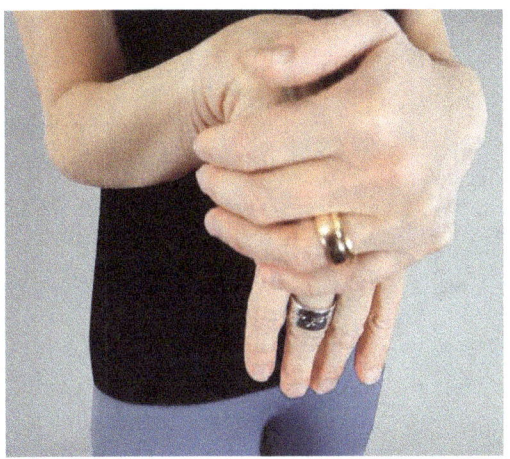

With one arm outstretched, put your palm facing downward; now, press that palm down with the fingers on the other hand. Hold for 10 seconds and relax. Repeat 5 times. This will help relieve tension on the palm side of the thumb joint that occurs when gripping needles or yarn too tightly.

Hand pull

Put both hands together and place them palm up on with fingers together without bending them at the base joint (where the finger meets your palm). Gently pull your hands apart until you feel a stretch in your fingers and palm - but do not push so hard that it hurts! Hold the position for 15 seconds, then relax for 30 seconds before repeating this stretch again if needed.

Hand Stretch

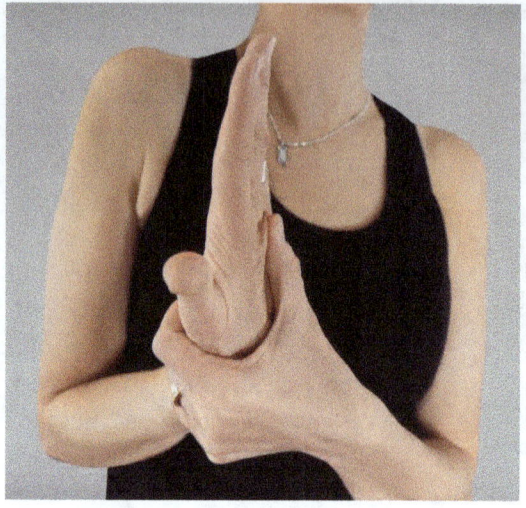

Hold your right hand out in front of you with the palm facing down. With your left hand, grab your right wrist and pull it back toward you until you feel a stretch in the palm of your right hand. Hold for 30 seconds, and then relax. Repeat 3 times on each side.

Forearm and Wrist Stretch

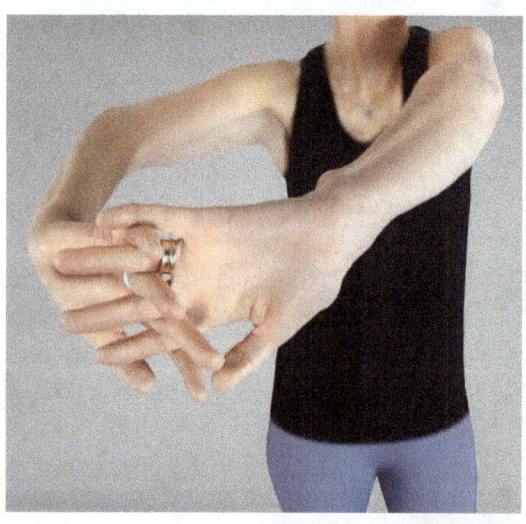

Hold both hands together with palms facing each other at chest height. Slowly raise both hands in front of you and stretch as far as they will go while keeping them together. Hold for 30 seconds, and then relax. Repeat 3 times on each side.

Sitting for too long

You may have heard that sitting is the new smoking or that too much sitting is bad for you. But what happens to your body when you're seated for too long?

Muscles can start to atrophy after being inactive for only 15 minutes. This means they begin to break down and lose their strength, which can lead to pain and injury. The lower back is one of the most common areas for this type of injury, as it's very difficult to maintain a strong core when you're sitting all day.

When you sit all day, blood flow slows down, and muscles become less flexible because there is no longer a need for them to work as hard. Sitting also puts pressure on your bladder and intestines, which can cause urinary tract infections (UTIs) or constipation if left untreated. Sitting too long also increases the risk of developing blood clots (deep vein thrombosis) and other circulation problems because blood pools in your legs rather than flowing through them.

The average American sits for eight hours a day. The human body is not designed to be seated for such long periods of time, which can cause a slew of health problems.

Sitting for long periods of time can cause pain and soreness in your lower back, hips, and thighs, as well as your neck, shoulders, and upper arms. This is because the body is designed to be active, not stationary. Even if you're fit and healthy, sitting still for hours puts stress on your body that it may not be able to handle.

Sitting also puts less pressure on your bones and joints than standing does, so your bones don't have as much support when you're sitting down compared to when you're standing up straight with good posture. This means that even if you have good posture while sitting down, it may still be bad for your bones because there's less support from gravity when you're not standing up straight.

If you're a person who spends a lot of time sitting down, you might be wondering why your back, butt, and legs often feel sore by the end of the day. This is because, after long periods of time, sitting can cause muscle fatigue in your lower back and hamstrings – the muscles that run along the backs of your thighs.

When you sit for an extended period of time without any movement, your back muscles become tight and stiff. This stiffness can pull on your hips and pelvis, causing pain or discomfort. Your hamstrings are commonly tight after sitting because they're shortened while you're seated. This causes them to pull on both the knee and ankle joints when standing up or walking, which can cause pain in those areas as well.

The first thing that you need to do is get up and walk around for 5 minutes every hour or so. If you're feeling pain or discomfort while sitting for too long, then try some of these exercises:

Leg raises

Lie on your back and use your leg muscles to raise your legs into the air. Hold them there for 3 seconds and then lower again slowly. Repeat 10 times per leg. This will help strengthen your core and back muscles.

Arm circles

Sit up straight in a chair and make sure that your shoulders are relaxed and down by your sides. Then move one arm out in front of you with your palm facing down and circle it around until it's back where it started (like you were making a circle with the palm of your hand). Do this 10 times on each side of your body – repeat 5 times if necessary until you feel better!

Cat-cow

This yoga pose increases mobility in your spine while also stretching out your abdomen muscles and relaxing tight shoulders and neck muscles from hunching over a computer all day long.

Shoulder blade squeeze

Take a deep breath through your nose while squeezing your shoulder blades together as if they were hugging each other behind your back. Hold for five seconds, then slowly release the breath out through your mouth while relaxing those muscles again

Walking

Walking is a huge part of daily life for many people. It can be used for exercise or as a means of transportation. Whether you're walking around the neighborhood or taking your dog out for a walk, physical activity is essential to keeping your body healthy.

Muscles are made up of bundles of muscle fibers that contract and relax to cause movement. When the muscles contract, they shorten and become tense. When they relax, they lengthen and become loose. This action causes the bones to move against each other, which is what makes your legs move when you walk or run. The more you walk and run, the stronger your muscles get at moving your bones and keeping them in place so that you can walk or run safely without falling down.

When you first start walking or running regularly, it takes time for your muscles to get used to being used this way every day. As a result, some people experience soreness in their legs after walking or running for a while because their muscles are not used to working out like this every day yet.

Soreness after walking or running can happen because of two reasons: either because the muscles were not strong enough to handle the activity yet or because there were too many repetitions of that particular activity done within a short period of time (overuse).

Walking is a low-impact exercise that uses your calves, quadriceps, hamstrings, and gluteal muscles. When you walk, your legs bend at the knee and hip joints, which causes these muscles to contract so that you can move forward. As you walk faster, the intensity of each muscle increases until they begin working hard enough to fatigue them. The quadriceps, which are located on the front of your thigh, are responsible for moving your lower leg away from your midline during walking.

The following are some of the muscle groups that walkers use when moving forward:

Hamstrings – These muscles are located on the back of your upper legs. They bend the knee and extend the hip. If you're walking slowly, you're using only one-quarter to one-half of your maximum hamstring strength. If you walk faster, however, you'll be using more of these muscles.

Quadriceps – These muscles are located on the front of your upper thighs and surround the kneecap (patella). To move forward while walking, you must flex your knees and straighten them again as part of each step.

Gluteus maximus and gluteus medius – These two large buttocks muscles act as stabilizers when you walk with good posture and balance (when they're functioning properly). They also help stabilize your pelvis when bending forward or backward while standing still or walking slowly; when walking faster, they help lift one leg out of its track after swinging past it.

Ankle circles

Stand on one foot and circle the ankle in both directions (clockwise and counterclockwise). Repeat 10 times, then switch feet.

Bench hamstring stretch

Stretching your hamstrings can help relieve tightness in your lower back area. This is an easy stretch to do while sitting down as well, so take advantage of those moments when you're stuck at a desk or resting between errands. You can do this stretch by putting one foot on your couch and leaning forward to reach your foot until you feel the stretch in your hamstrings.

Quadriceps stretch

Stand facing away from a wall about two feet away, with one leg bent behind you at a 90-degree angle and your ankle on the floor. Hold on to something sturdy if needed, then slowly lean forward until you feel the tension in front of your hip; hold for 15 seconds and repeat 10 times per side.

Calf stretch

Stand up straight with knees slightly bent and put both hands on a wall or countertop in front of you; you should feel this stretch in the backs of your legs where they meet your calves (not necessarily where they attach). Keep one foot flat on the floor while leaning forward until you feel the tension in that calf muscle; hold for 15 seconds and repeat 10 times per side.

Knee-to-chest stretch

Lie flat on your back with both knees bent, and raise one leg toward your chest until you feel a stretch in the front of that thigh muscle. Hold for 30 seconds, then repeat on the other side.

Going up the stairs

If you're like most people, the stairs are a part of your daily life. You use them to go up and down from your bedroom, kitchen, basement, or garage. But how often do you think about the effect that walking up and down the stairs has on your muscles?

The answer is that it's a lot.

Walking up stairs uses more muscle groups than walking on flat ground or even going up an incline in a wheelchair. And if you do it frequently, it can lead to some muscle imbalances that can cause pain and discomfort.

When you walk upstairs, your legs are in constant motion; they support your body weight as you rise and fall with each step.

Your hip flexors – which pull your thighs toward your abdomen – contract forcefully to help raise each leg upward while maintaining balance and stability.

Your quadriceps – which straighten the knee – contract forcefully to lift each foot off the step before placing it again on the next step above (or below). This action occurs every time you take a step forward with one leg while keeping the other foot planted firmly on the same level step or stair tread as before.

Walking up the stairs makes muscles sore, but it's not because you're overstressing them. Instead, it's because you're activating your leg muscles in a different way than usual – and they need time to adjust. When we walk, we typically use our quads, but when we climb stairs, our glutes and hamstrings are doing more of the work.

The muscles in your legs have different roles. Your quadriceps, your hamstrings, and your gluteus maximus all work together to bend and straighten your knees. But when you climb an incline – like a flight of stairs – those same muscles play two additional roles: They help rotate the hips inward and outward so that each leg swings forward and backward as you step up or down. And they help stabilize the knee joint as it moves through its full range of motion. After climbing the stairs, it's always good to perform these stretches:

Standing quad stretch

Stand on one leg with the other leg bent behind you, your foot flat on the floor. Lean forward and push your hips back until you feel a stretch in the front of your thigh. Hold for 15 seconds, then switch legs.

Side leg stretch

Sit on the floor with one leg extended in front of you and one bent at the knee so that it's near your chest. Reach for the stretched-out leg with the corresponding hand for support as you lean sideways until you feel a stretch in your hamstring tendons behind your thigh. Hold for 20 seconds, then switch legs.

Quadriceps stretch

While lying on the floor, bend one leg at the knee and place the foot flat on the floor while extending the other leg behind you with the knee straightened out as far as possible without straining yourself. Raise your hips upward (you should feel this in your quadriceps muscles). Hold for 20-30 seconds before lowering down slowly. Repeat this position 2-3 times.

Chapter 6: Pinpoint Focus: The Hips

We've all been there before. You're sitting in front of the TV, and you feel a dull ache in your hips. Maybe it's from sitting too long, or maybe it's just from spending hours every day with your feet pointed out and your knees bent – as many of us do when we're driving, working at a desk, or sitting on an airplane.

Whatever the reason, hip pain is a common complaint among Americans, especially for those over 40. And it can be difficult to pinpoint exactly what's causing the discomfort. Oftentimes, it's due to tight muscles that aren't getting enough attention during exercise (such as hamstrings and glutes). Other times, it's caused by weak muscles that need more exercise than they're getting (like quadriceps).

The hips are a complex ball-and-socket joint that is subject to a great deal of stress. The hip joint allows you to raise your leg to walk, run, jump and climb stairs. It also allows you to twist your body from side to side and bend forward at the waist.

The hip flexor muscles connect the front of your pelvis to your thigh bone. They help you bend forward at the waist and lift your knee toward your chest when you walk or run. If these muscles become tight or shortened, they can pull on the pelvis, causing misalignment in both hips. This can lead to pain in the lower back or groin area as well as problems with walking and running properly.

Because these movements take place in a relatively small area of your body, stretching is important for keeping this joint flexible and healthy. In addition, stretching will help relieve back pain by improving circulation and strengthening muscles around the spine. Hip pain can be a common problem among seniors, and it's important to know what might be causing it.

According to the National Institute on Aging (NIA), hip pain is one of the most common reasons why people visit a doctor. About 4 in 10 adults aged 65 and older have experienced hip pain at some point in their lives.

Hip pain is a common condition that can affect people of all ages. It can be caused by several different issues, including arthritis, muscle strains, tears, falls, sports injuries, and more. Hip pain may result in a disability that limits your ability to do activities of daily living (ADLs), such as walking or climbing stairs. Hip pain can make you feel like you need to sit down or lie down all the time. You might also experience a dull ache in your hips when standing up after sitting for long periods.

If you're an elderly person with hip pain, there are several possible causes why you may have it. Osteoarthritis or wear-and-tear arthritis is the most common cause of hip pain in seniors. This type of arthritis occurs when the cartilage that cushions your joints breaks down over time, causing them to become inflamed and painful. It often affects both hips at once but can also affect just one side of your body at a time.

Many people who suffer from hip pain experience some level of disability from their condition, but there are ways to manage the pain and prevent it from interfering with your daily life. If your hip pain is severe enough to significantly limit your mobility and quality of life, then it's important to see your doctor right away so they can determine the cause and recommend appropriate treatment options.

In any case, stretching can help loosen up tight muscles in the hips so they don't pull on other areas of your body – which can lead to pain. So if you sit all day long like most people do these days, do yourself a favor and add these moves into your routine!

Side lunge

Stand straight with feet shoulder-width apart, toes pointing forward and knees slightly bent. Step to the side with one foot and lower your body until both knees form 90-degree angles, then push back up to the start position.

Bending over stretch

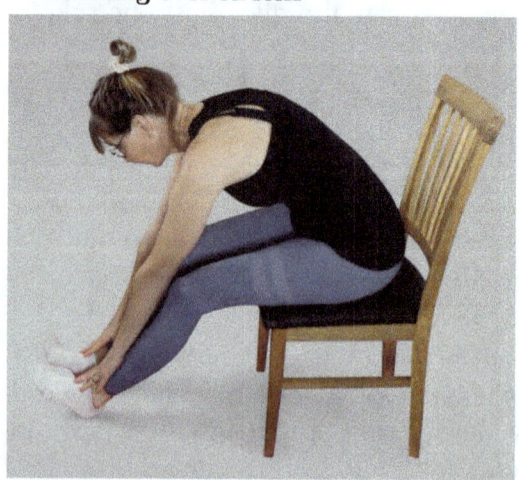

Sit down on a chair or couch and bend over to reach out for the feet. If this stretch seems difficult, try reaching out for your knees instead. Hold position 10-20 seconds and repeat 2 times.

Lunge Stretch

Stand upright with your feet together. Take a big step forward with the left foot, bending both knees until both knees are at 90-degree angles. Your left knee should be directly over your left ankle, and your right knee should be directly over your right ankle. Lean forward slightly, keeping your back straight, and grab hold of bent knees in front of you while your other leg is stretched out behind you and touching the floor. Hold the stretch for 10 seconds, then switch sides and repeat.

Hip Flexor Stretch

While standing, place one foot in front of you and the other one back in the lunge position. Straighten your back leg (but don't let it touch the floor) while bending your front leg. Place the hand opposite your bent leg on the floor for balance and slowly raise your other hand, pointing to the sky.

Maintain this position for 15 seconds, then slowly return to an upright position without allowing any bouncing movement when coming back up into a standing position again. Perform three sets of 10 repetitions per side before moving on to another exercise variation like the next one listed below!

Standing forward fold

Stand with feet shoulder-width apart and toes turned out slightly (your big toe should point in). Bend forward from the hips until you feel a stretch in your hamstrings. Hold for 15 seconds, then straighten up and repeat once more before repeating the entire sequence once more.

Chapter 7: Pinpoint Focus: Neck and Shoulders

Neck pain is a common problem among seniors, and it can be caused by a variety of factors. The neck is a complicated region that consists of several bones, ligaments, and joints. The muscles, nerves, and discs that support the head are contained within this area. The neck contains many blood vessels, including the spinal cord, which runs from the brain to the base of the spine.

When we are young, our necks are flexible enough to allow us to turn our heads from side to side without experiencing any pain or discomfort in our necks. As we age, however, our necks become stiffer, causing them to lose their flexibility which can lead to pain when turning your head from side to side. In addition, as you age, your discs become less elastic, causing a decrease in the range of motion in your neck.

The following are some of the most common causes of neck pain in seniors:

Cervical spondylosis- The cervical spine consists of seven vertebrae stacked one on top of another. As you age, bony projections (spurs) can develop on these vertebrae, which can cause pressure on nerves and other structures in the back of your neck. Pain from cervical spondylosis usually occurs in your upper back between your shoulder blades.

Arthritis- Arthritis is a degenerative joint disease that causes inflammation and damage to the joints. While osteoarthritis, or "wear-and-tear" arthritis, typically affects older adults, rheumatoid arthritis, which is an autoimmune disorder, can affect people of all ages, including children and young adults. Both types of arthritis can cause stiffness and limit mobility in the joints throughout the body – including those in your neck.

Whiplash- When there's an accident or sudden movement that stretches or tears ligaments and muscles around the joint, it can cause whiplash, which often results in headaches and stiffness in the back and neck. This type of injury typically occurs when someone hits their head against something hard – for example, during a car crash – but it can also happen when someone falls down stairs or off a ladder.

Tendinitis- Tendons are the fibrous cords that connect muscles to bones, allowing us to move our joints and limbs. Tendinitis occurs when tendons become inflamed from overuse or injury.

Fibromyalgia- Fibromyalgia is a chronic disorder characterized by widespread muscle pain and tenderness, fatigue, sleep disturbances, cognitive difficulties, and depression. It can cause pain throughout the body but is felt most strongly in the shoulders, back, and hips.

Scoliosis (curvature of the spine)- Scoliosis occurs when one side of your spine develops a curve that looks like an "S" shape or a "C" shape. In severe cases, scoliosis can cause severe neck and back pain that worsens as you get older because it changes how your spine functions naturally with age.

Disc degeneration- Discs are small shock-absorbing cushions between the vertebrae (the bones that make up your spine). When you're young, they're strong and healthy, but as you get older, they can wear away and start to bulge or even break down, causing pain along your spine.

Spinal stenosis- Spinal stenosis is a narrowing of the spaces within your spinal cord that compresses nerves in your back and neck area, causing severe pain, numbness, or weakness in your arms or legs as well as difficulty walking or turning over in bed due to weakness in your hip muscles (sciatica).

If you have neck pain, stretching can be an important part of your treatment. Stretching increases flexibility in the muscles and tendons around your neck and upper back. This helps reduce tightness in those areas, which can lead to pain. When you experience neck pain, it's important to be proactive and take action to prevent the problem from getting worse.

Here are some easy exercises you can do at home:

Neck rolls

This simple exercise helps relax the muscles in your neck by stretching them out. Starting from a standing position, slowly roll your head from side to side, feeling the stretch in your neck and shoulders. Repeat 10 times on each side.

Upper back and shoulder stretch

Bend sideways at the waist, keeping your knees straight and legs slightly open. Lock your hands and reach sideways in the same direction as your core – while keeping your arms straight and shoulder blades down throughout this exercise. Hold this position for 30 seconds before returning to an upright position and repeating it three times on each side.

Chest opener

Stand with feet shoulder-width apart as you cross raise both arms behind your head while keeping them locked together. Gently pull back on the arms as if trying to open a door behind you until you feel a stretch along your chest wall and shoulder blade area – hold this position for 30 seconds before returning to an upright position and repeating it three times on each side.

Chapter 8: Pinpoint Focus: Knees, Ankles & Feet

Knee pain is a common complaint among older adults and affects approximately 20% of people aged 65 and older. The knee joint is a hinge joint that allows your leg to bend and straighten. It also allows your entire leg to rotate as you walk or run. The good news is that most cases of knee pain in seniors are not serious.

Osteoarthritis is the most common type of arthritis, but it's not inevitable with age. Osteoarthritis is a degenerative joint disease that affects the cartilage in your knee joints. As the cartilage deteriorates, it leads to bone rubbing against bone. This friction can cause inflammation and swelling around the knee, which leads to pain and stiffness. Osteoarthritis is more common as people age, but it can also occur earlier due to injury or other factors such as obesity or excessive exercise.

Arthritis is a term used for more than 100 types of joint conditions that cause inflammation, pain, and stiffness in the joints – including osteoarthritis. You may hear these conditions referred to as degenerative joint diseases because they involve deterioration of the cartilage in your joints. Rheumatoid arthritis is another condition that causes arthritis in the knees. It's an autoimmune disease in which the immune system attacks healthy tissue, including cartilage, causing inflammation and pain in joints.

Chondromalacia (also known as runner's knee) occurs when there's damage to the articular cartilage underneath the kneecap from overuse or injury, leading to friction between it and the thigh bone during movement. This causes pain and swelling around your patella tendon attachment point on your tibia bone (top of the shin). Stretching exercises can help loosen up your muscles, joints, and tendons. They also relieve stress on your knees by increasing flexibility and mobility in your hips and legs.

The right stretches for you will depend on your age and health history. It's important to talk with a doctor before starting any exercise routine – especially if you have a chronic condition such as arthritis or diabetes that affects your joints. There are several easy stretches that can help relieve knee pain. These are just a few:

Prayer Pose

This is an effective stretch for the quadriceps and hip flexors. To do it, kneel on a mat with your hands placed on either side of your feet. Bend at the waist, bringing your chest toward your knees while keeping your back straight. Hold this position for 30 seconds to one minute.

Knee flexor stretch

This involves bending forward and grabbing your knee with your hand. You then pull your knee forward toward your buttock slowly until you feel a stretch in the front of your thigh, which is where your quadriceps muscles are located. Hold this position for 20 seconds and do this three times on each side of the body.

Hamstring stretch

Lie down on your back with both legs straight out in front of you on the floor. Bend one leg at a 90-degree angle with the foot flat on the floor and bring your hands behind that knee to grab it from underneath (not behind). Pull gently toward your chest until you feel a gentle stretch in your hamstring muscle group (the large muscle group on the back of each thigh). Hold for 15 to 20 seconds, then repeat with the other leg.

Knee circles

This involves standing up straight with both feet firmly planted on the floor. Slowly bend your knees and place each hand on the corresponding knee (you should feel a stretch in the front of the thigh). Make circles with your knees 5-10 times.

Wall-Assisted Quad Stretch

This stretch is an easy way to open up your hips and hamstrings while helping to relieve knee pain. Do this stretch after a run or any time you're feeling tight in your quads.

Stand with your back against a wall and place your right foot on the ground a couple of inches away from the wall. Bend your left leg at the knee so that it's parallel to the floor, and place both hands on top of your left thigh just above where it joins your pelvis. Make sure that both knees are pointing straight ahead; do not allow them to bend inward toward each other.

Lean forward slightly into your right hip until you feel a comfortable stretch in your left hip and quadriceps muscle (right thigh). Hold for 15 seconds, then switch sides and repeat for three sets on each leg.

Kneeling Lunge

This is a great stretch for your knees. Start in a kneeling position with your feet together and your hands on the floor. Step one foot forward, keeping your hips square to the front of the mat, and lower down until you feel a stretch in the front of that thigh. Keep your back knee on the ground, or you can place it on a pillow or mat if you need additional support. If you have any pain in your kneecap, do not let it rest directly on the floor. Hold for 20 seconds on each side.

Ankle pain, on the other hand, can be caused by many things, including overuse (such as running for long distances), injury (such as rolling your ankle), or a medical condition. While it's important to see a doctor if you have any concerns about the cause of your pain, you can help relieve ankle pain by doing simple stretches several times a day.

The most common cause of ankle pain is an injury to the ankle ligaments. Ligaments are bands of tissue that connect bone to bone, and they help stabilize your joint. Injury to an ankle ligament can happen when you twist or roll the ankle or step off a curb too fast. This type of injury often causes swelling, bruising, and pain.

A second common cause of ankle pain is arthritis, which is inflammation of one or more joints in the body. Arthritis can also affect other joints besides the ankles, including wrists, knees, and hips. If you have ankle pain, it's important to identify the cause of your symptoms so you can get the right treatment. Here are some of the most common causes of ankle pain:

Overuse – Overuse injuries occur when you put too much stress on a joint or tissue without allowing it time to recover. This can lead to inflammation, swelling, and other damage in the area. Common examples include the runner's knee, shin splints, and plantar fasciitis (heel pain).

Trauma – Traumatic injuries often result from falls or direct blows to the joint, causing bruising, bleeding, and swelling around the area. It's important not to try walking on an injured ankle right away because doing so could make things worse by putting more stress on the joint than it can handle. If possible, elevate your foot above heart level for about an hour after an injury occurs until any bleeding stops completely.

Sprains and strains – An ankle sprain occurs when you overstretch or tear the ligaments that support your ankle joint. A strained ligament is torn partially but not completely through. An ankle strain occurs when the muscles, tendons, or other soft tissue around your ankle joint are damaged by overuse or injury.

Bursitis and tendonitis – Overuse injuries can cause inflammation of bursae – small fluid-filled sacs that cushion the bones, tendons, and muscles around joints – resulting in bursitis. Tendonitis is inflammation of tendons, which are fibrous cords that connect muscle to bone. These conditions can also be caused by repetitive stress on an area of your body over time, such as standing on hard surfaces all day long, walking on uneven terrain, or hiking outdoors with friends.

Diabetes Mellitus – Diabetes mellitus is a condition in which blood glucose levels are too high due to a problem with insulin production or use by cells throughout the body. The more common type of diabetes mellitus among older adults is Type 2 diabetes mellitus (T2DM), which accounts for more than 90 percent of all cases of diabetes in this age group. T2DM may affect your circulation and cause nerve damage that leads to poor blood flow to your feet – including your ankles – which can lead to problems such as peripheral neuropathy.

Here are some stretches you can do to help relieve ankle pain and increase mobility.

Heel drop

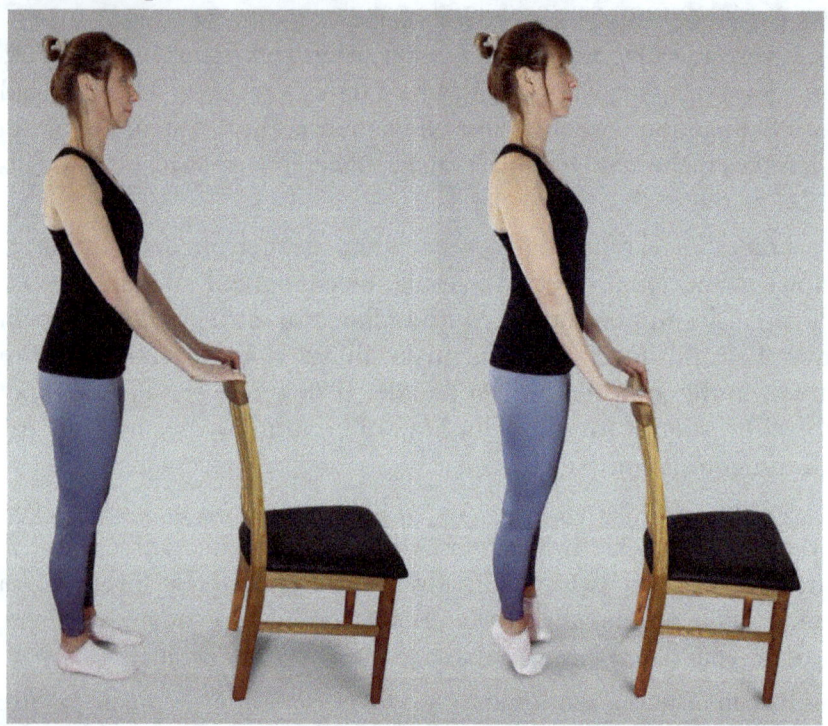

Keep your legs straight and hold on to a chair for balance. Drop your heel down toward the floor by bending your knee as far as possible without pain. Hold for 10 seconds, then repeat with the opposite leg forward three times on each side.

Supine Ankle Stretch

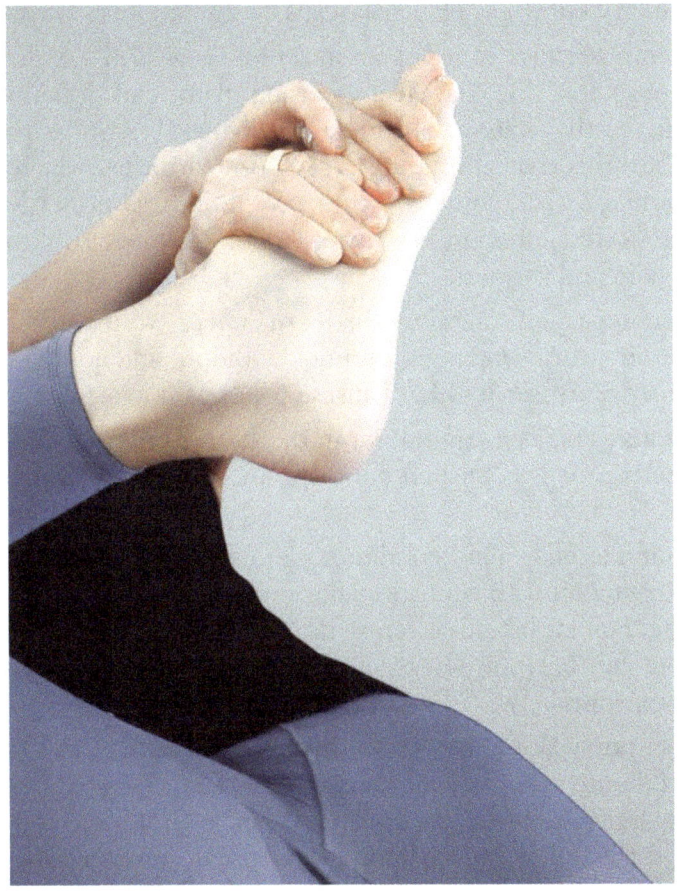

Lie on the ground while lying on your back with one leg straight and the other bent at 90 degrees. Pull your bent foot with your until you feel a stretch, then hold for 20 seconds. Repeat three times on each side.

And last but not least is foot pain. Foot pain in older adults can be caused by many things, including arthritis and joint problems.

The joints of the foot are made up of small bones called phalanges. These bones are held together by ligaments – strong bands of tissue that connect bones at a joint. The ligaments help support your foot while also allowing it to move forward and backward, as well as side to side.

When you walk or run, your feet undergo tremendous pressure from the weight of your body. If you have weak ligaments in your feet, they may tear more easily under this pressure. The result is a painful injury known as plantar fasciitis.

A common cause of foot pain in seniors is arthritis. Arthritis can affect the joints in your feet, causing pain and inflammation, according to the National Institute on Aging. The most common type of arthritis that affects the feet is osteoarthritis, which occurs when cartilage wears away over time. Without this protective layer between bones, pressure is increased and bones rub together, causing pain and stiffness.

Other types of arthritis that can affect your feet include rheumatoid arthritis (an autoimmune condition) and gout (a form of inflammatory arthritis). Other causes of foot pain in seniors include:

Bunions- This is a painful bump on the big toe joint that occurs when the big toe gets pushed out of position as it rubs against other toes.

Plantar fasciitis- This condition causes heel pain and stiffness when pushing off with your toes after waking up or after sitting for a long time. Plantar fasciitis often starts as mild discomfort in the early stages but can become severe enough to limit daily activities if not treated appropriately.

Bony spurs- Bony spurs are small bumps that form along the edges of bones where bone meets the bone. They happen when cartilage wears away from bone surfaces over time, creating an uneven surface that causes friction and pressure on nearby nerves and tendons. Bony spurs can form anywhere in your body – including your feet – but they're more common at certain joints than others. They can also develop after an injury to a joint or tendon if you have a genetic predisposition for them or if you have diabetes.

Stretching is one of the most effective ways to relieve foot pain. The following stretches target specific areas of your feet and legs to help loosen tight muscles and improve flexibility.

Massage your feet with a rolling pin or foam roller

Start by massaging each foot with a rolling pin or foam roller for two minutes, then roll over each section of your foot for 30 seconds. Massage your toes, heels, and arches using a tennis ball, golf ball, or another hard object: Apply pressure to each section of your foot by bending at the ankle while rolling over it with one hand using a tennis ball, golf ball, or another hard object.

Toe stretch

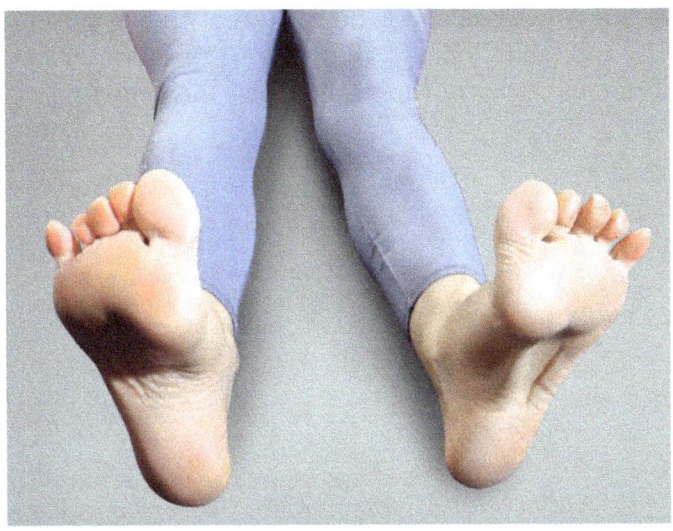

Sit down while keeping your body and legs straight. Stretch out your toes as far apart from each other as possible. Keep the position for 15 seconds before resting. Repeat 2-3 times.

Calf Stretch

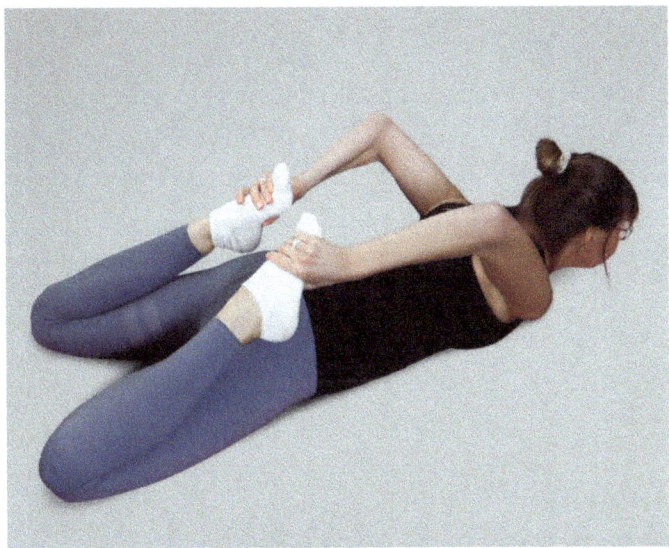

The calf muscle runs along the back of your lower leg from the top of your ankle to just below the knee. If tightness in this muscle is contributing to foot pain, try this stretch. Lye down with your belly. Grab feet with each corresponding hand and pull them to your buttocks to feel a pull on your calves and foot.

Slowly lower yourself back down to the starting position when you feel comfortable doing so without losing balance or feeling any discomfort in either leg or hip joints; repeat this exercise.

Chapter 9: Stretching Properly

In this chapter, we will discuss the importance of stretching properly. This is because when you do not stretch properly, you end up doing more harm than good to your body. If you're trying to improve flexibility, it can be tempting to stretch your entire body all at once. But if you want to get the most out of your stretches, it's best to target them to the areas that need it most.

The best way to approach flexibility training is by using a variety of different stretching movements. But when you're trying to stretch, it's easy to do the wrong stretches or even hurt yourself by stretching too far. So how do you know which stretches are right for you? Start by figuring out where you need more flexibility. Then choose stretches that target those areas, says physical therapist Erin Hausenblas, DPT, who works at Ohio State University's Wexner Medical Center in Columbus, Ohio.

If you're unsure of what stretches are best for you, consult with a professional fitness trainer who can evaluate your fitness level and recommend stretches that are safe yet effective for your goals. It's a common misconception that stretching is just about flexibility.

If you've been sitting on a couch all day and have lost your "squatting groove," or if you're just getting back into a fitness routine after a long break, it's important to start with proper stretching form.

Of course, some people are naturally more flexible than others, but you can still improve your flexibility with practice. Don't be discouraged if your flexibility is poor - there is hope! Improving your stretching form is a process that can take time, and nobody can become an expert overnight. But here are some tips for getting started:

Stretch regularly

Daily or a few times per week is best. How often you should stretch is determined by your fitness level, goals, and injury history. Some people find that they need to stretch more often than others, depending on their workout schedule, level of activity, and lifestyle.

If you're just starting with a stretching routine, you should probably do it at least once per day. This will help prevent soreness and increase circulation in your body. As time goes on, you'll find that you only need to stretch every other day or so to maintain your flexibility gains.

If you're new to fitness or haven't done much stretching before, start by doing some light aerobic activity such as walking or bicycling for 10 minutes each day. Stretch 20 minutes after each aerobic session for two weeks before moving on to more intense workouts like running or weightlifting. If you already have an established fitness routine but aren't used to stretching regularly, add 20 minutes of stretching after each workout for two weeks before moving on to more intense workouts.

Stretching should be done regularly before and after physical activity, as well as during breaks during daily work like gardening and cleaning. You should also stretch if you're feeling stiff or sore from sitting for a long time. You don't need any equipment or training to do stretches - just your body and some floor space. Stretching before exercise will warm up your muscles, making them more flexible. After exercise, stretching helps relieve muscle soreness.

Stretch in the morning before starting your day and again in the evening before going to bed. This also helps reduce stress throughout the day because it's easier to be calm when your muscles are loose than when they're tight.

Do NOT Bounce

Stretch gently and slowly without bouncing or forcing any part of your body beyond its natural range of motion. When it comes to stretching, the key is to hold each stretch for at least 15 seconds before moving on to another one. This will allow your muscles enough time to relax and lengthen before you try to stretch them further.

If you bounce during a stretch, however, you're preventing your muscles from relaxing and lengthening because they're constantly being stimulated by the motion. As such, bouncing during a stretch could lead to muscle tears and strains rather than helping with flexibility.

Bouncing while stretching can be harmful to your body and cause you to feel sore after exercising – more than you normally would have if you hadn't bounced at all! It causes microtears in your muscles. When we stretch, our bodies naturally tighten up in response to the threat of being stretched past their current limits. This is a natural self-protection mechanism that allows us to avoid injury by preventing us from going too far too fast when exercising or playing sports.

When we bounce while stretching, however, we force our muscles to relax, which then makes it easier for them to tear when they've stretched beyond their normal limits again (and again). This results in temporary pain associated with muscle soreness and inflammation but also long-term damage if it happens enough times over time because our bodies don't heal as quickly as they did when we were younger and more active!

Hold each stretch for 10-30 seconds

After holding a stretch, relax afterward for one minute or more before repeating it. That way, your muscles will have time to relax between stretches, so they don't get sore when you hold them longer. This encourages your muscles to relax and lengthen, which can help improve your flexibility. If you feel like you're having trouble breathing or are straining too much to keep your body in position, take it down a notch until you can hold the stretch without any discomfort.

Stretch both sides of your body equally. Hold each side for the same amount of seconds for both sides of your body. This ensures that you're getting balanced stretching throughout your body instead of just one side at a time. However, if you feel constant pain when stretching, stop immediately and consult your doctor or physiotherapist before continuing any exercise program.

Avoid overstretching

Overstretching can cause injuries like muscle tears or tendinitis if you're trying to become too flexible too fast and if you are pushing beyond what's safe for your body type and current fitness level. You might have heard that if you stretch enough, you can avoid injury. But the reality is that stretching makes you more susceptible to injury.

If your muscles are stretched beyond their capacity, they become weak and unable to contract properly. The result is muscle weakness, poor posture, and joint pain. If you want to stretch before exercising, make sure it's not too long before your workout begins - ideally, no more than 15 minutes beforehand. Stretching too close to exercise can weaken your muscles even further and make them less responsive during your workout.

If you are just stretching your muscles, stick to short sessions of static stretching (where a muscle is held in an elongated position for at least 30 seconds). Static stretches are better than ballistic (or dynamic) stretches if you are not doing a workout session afterward because they don't require any momentum from the body part being stretched. This means they're safer than ballistic stretches and less likely to cause damage or injury when performed incorrectly.

Breathe deeply as you stretch

Focus on taking slow breaths through your nose as you exhale out of your mouth. This will help relax your muscles, so they're more pliable when you're stretching them out. Breathing while stretching has many benefits, including helping to relax the mind and body and improving circulation to muscles being stretched. Breathing properly during stretching can also help you avoid injury during exercise by allowing you to focus on the task at hand rather than your breathing.

When you breathe properly during stretching, you will be able to concentrate more on what you are trying to accomplish with your body rather than struggling with how much air you are taking in or holding onto as you stretch. For example, if you are trying to maintain proper posture while stretching your back muscles, breathing correctly will allow you to stay focused on maintaining this posture instead of worrying about whether or not your breath is being held for too long or not long enough for optimal results.

There are several different ways that people choose to breathe while performing stretches, but there are two main techniques that most people use: abdominal breathing and thoracic breathing.

Abdominal breathing is a great way to stay calm and relaxed. It's also useful for stretching, as it helps you get deeper into a stretch. The most important thing is to breathe deeply from your abdomen rather than just your upper chest. To do this, imagine someone is pressing down on your upper chest with their hands, and you're trying to push them away. This will help you breathe more deeply into your abdominal muscles and not just your chest.

On each in-breath, relax as much as possible and allow yourself to expand as much as possible. On each out-breath, contract your abdominal muscles so that they pull in towards the spine (think of sucking inwards towards your spine). You can practice this technique anywhere at any time, even when you're walking around or waiting for something!

Thoracic breathing is also an essential part of any stretching session. It's also a great way to loosen up tight muscles and joints, as well as calm your mind and help you focus on the task at hand: stretching! The idea behind thoracic breathing is to fill your lungs with air from the bottom up rather than from the top down.

Take a deep breath through your nose, filling your diaphragm. Your stomach should expand first, followed by your chest and then your neck. Your shoulders should not rise much higher than they normally do when you breathe normally.

Once you've taken a full breath in through your nose, exhale slowly through pursed lips or by gently blowing out air through pursed lips. You should feel like you're pushing everything out of your lungs as you exhale completely – including all of the air in them (as opposed to just blowing out some of it). Repeat this process until you feel comfortable with it, then continue with whatever stretch or exercise you were doing before adding this step into the mix.

Never hold your breath while stretching

If you're not breathing during a stretch, you're increasing the risk of injury. Holding your breath while stretching can cause what's known as a Valsalva maneuver. This is when you force yourself to exhale forcefully against a closed throat (as if trying to blow out a candle). It's similar to what happens when you have to bear down and push a bowel movement out.

The Valsalva maneuver can cause an increase in blood pressure and an increase in abdominal pressure that puts pressure on your spine. When this happens, your spine has no other choice but to flex (bend) - which could lead to muscle strain or, worse, a disc herniation (when part of the spinal disc ruptures through its outer covering).

Stretching without breathing is also dangerous because it causes increased blood flow away from your muscles and into your arms, neck, and face - areas that aren't prepared to handle the extra blood flow that comes with holding your breath. The result? Redness or even bruising in these areas after stretching.

Stretching an injured muscle is usually a bad idea

It can prolong the healing process and even cause additional injury. Instead, you should rest the injured area to allow it to heal. The most common reason people stretch an injured muscle is because they believe it will help them feel better right away. The truth is that stretching can make an injury worse by increasing your risk of tearing or straining the muscle further.

When you stretch out a muscle, it causes your body to release endorphins, which are hormones that produce a sense of euphoria and well-being. Unfortunately, this rush of endorphins can make you feel better temporarily but also masks any pain from an injury and makes it harder for your brain to tell if something is wrong with your body. It's like taking painkillers for a headache - they might make you feel better temporarily but won't cure whatever is causing the pain in the first place.

When you stretch, your body starts to repair the damage caused by the injury. When you do a static stretch, which is the type most people do, you're restricting blood flow to the injured area. This causes pain and inflammation as your body tries to get rid of all that extra blood.

In addition, when you stretch a muscle with an injury, it can cause more damage if your tissue is already weak and damaged. You're not just putting unnecessary stress on your muscles – you're putting unnecessary stress on your bones too!

If you have knee pain that doesn't go away with rest, it's time to see a doctor. Pain is part of the body's natural warning system. It's something our bodies use to tell us something isn't right. If something hurts, it needs attention.

The doctor will ask about your past medical history and your symptoms. He or she will also do a physical exam and may order x-rays or other tests if needed. The doctor can determine if there are any problems with the bones, muscles, tendons, or ligaments surrounding the area that continuously hurts.

If you're looking for ways to make your stretching more enjoyable, consider foam rolling. This simple technique targets the muscles you've been working on while also providing relief from soreness and tightness.

Foam rolling is a form of self-myofascial release that involves rolling over a foam cylinder with your body weight. The technique can be used on any muscle group, although foam rollers are usually designed specifically for different parts of the body, such as hamstrings, quads, and calves.

Foam rolling is an excellent way to improve your stretching routine. It also helps relieve muscle soreness and increase flexibility in the muscles being rolled on. Many people who stretch regularly also foam roll to achieve additional benefits. This is because foam rolling helps break down tightness in the muscles, which can improve flexibility and reduce the risk of injury.

Foam rolling is often used pre-or post-workout, but it can also be done at any time during the day. The best way to use foam rolling is to find a position that's comfortable for you, then roll up and down your muscle groups in slow, controlled movements until you feel soreness. If this doesn't happen after 10 seconds or so, move on to another spot on your body.

These rollers improve circulation by increasing blood flow to the muscle fibers and surrounding tissues, which aids in the removal of toxins and waste products from the cells. The increased circulation also helps bring oxygen and nutrients to the muscles for repair after exercise.

Yoga mats are also necessary for a better stretching experience. They prevent slipping and protect your body from the hard floor or studio flooring. Yoga mats come in a variety of shapes, sizes, thicknesses, and textures. The most common types of yoga mats are made from PVC or rubber and are called "sticky" mats because they tend to stay put on the floor. There are also non-sticky mats made from natural rubber or jute that offer more traction than sticky mats but may not stay in place as well on carpeted floors.

The best yoga mat for you depends on your personal preferences and needs. Consider your flexibility level and whether you prefer a thicker or thinner mat, how much money you want to spend, and what features are important to you when choosing the right mat for you.

Yoga mats provide much-needed cushioning for your knees, elbows, hips, back, and other joints. If you practice on the floor, the mat will protect your body from the hardwood or concrete beneath it and prevent injuries such as bruising or sprained joints. The padding also helps absorb sweat during vigorous workouts like Bikram yoga, making it easier to maintain proper form throughout your session.

They also prevent slipping. Many people think that yoga is all about balance – but even if you're pretty good at standing on one leg without falling over, slipping around during poses can be embarrassing and downright dangerous for your body. A good yoga mat provides traction, so you don't slip and fall while attempting complicated stretches.

Another great accessory to include in your stretching routine are ankle weights. These weights provide a simple and effective way to increase strength and improve balance. They can also be used for a wide range of exercises, from squats to lunges to calf raises. The added resistance helps develop the muscles in your ankles and lower legs, making them stronger and more capable of supporting your body weight.

Ankle weights are ideal for toning your lower body because they target specific muscle groups in the ankles, calves, knees, and thighs. In addition to increasing strength and improving coordination, they also improve flexibility by stretching muscles that support the joints during exercise.

Using ankle weights during stretches can help reduce injuries caused by overworking certain muscle groups while underusing others. When you strengthen weaker muscle groups through stretching with ankle weights, you'll reduce the risk of injury caused by imbalances between opposing muscle groups that often occur when one group is stronger than another.

They can even help improve your overall strength and conditioning. By working out with ankle weights, you will be able to improve your overall strength and conditioning more quickly than if you were doing the same stretching without them. This is because the added weight increases the intensity of each stretch, forcing your muscles to work harder to perform it correctly.

Most ankle weights are made of plastic or rubber materials that are durable enough for repeated use but still lightweight enough to be comfortable when worn around your ankles. Some models feature reflective designs, so you can see them even at night so you won't trip over them.

Accessory tools can make stretching easier and more fun (especially if they're colorful!). They often come with step-by-step instructions that guide you through each move – which makes them easier to learn than traditional stretches. And because they're usually made from lightweight materials such as plastic or foam rubber, they won't feel bulky in your hands or on your feet like a towel might feel when you wrap them around yourself for a hamstring stretch.

They're portable – so you can take them with you wherever you go! That means no matter where your yoga class takes place (in an office conference room, your living room floor, or even outside).

Chapter 10: Upping your Game

Once you get the hang of stretching consistently, it becomes second nature. Here are some routines that will help you become a pro:

Pre-Workout Stretch Routine

Squat Position

Squatting is a great way to warm up your body and prepare it for exercise. It can also be used as a pre-workout stretch or warm-up.

Perform squats as part of your warm-up routine before any physical activity, including running, biking, and strength training. To get started, place your feet shoulder-width apart with your toes pointed slightly outward. Keep your head up and back straight during the squatting process. Lower yourself by bending at the hips until your thighs are parallel to the floor (or lower if you can). Then stand back up again.

Squats work several major muscle groups, including quads, glutes, and hamstrings – all important muscle groups that should be warmed up before exercising so they can perform at their best during workouts.

Shoulder Squeeze

The Shoulder Squeeze is a great stretch for the shoulders. It can be done before or after your workout. The goal is to get your shoulders to open up and relax so that you can move more freely during your workout.

Stand with your feet hip distance apart or sit on a chair and hands by your sides. Take a deep breath through your nose. As you breathe out, drop your shoulders down, away from your ears, and toward the ground. At the same time, lift up on the balls of your feet and pull in toward each other to activate your glutes. Hold this position as you continue breathing deeply into your lower belly for three to four breaths (or more if needed). When finished, slowly release back into the starting position.

Arm Circles

One of the most common pre-workout stretches is arm circles. This simple move can help you prepare your body for a workout and also help prevent injury.

Arm circles are performed by holding your arms straight out in front of you, palms facing the ground. Slowly move them in a small circle, first clockwise, then counterclockwise. Repeat five or six times total to warm up your shoulders and upper back muscles.

Doing this stretch as part of your pre-workout routine helps loosen up tight muscles that can cause pain during exercise. It also increases blood flow to those muscles, which helps them perform better during activity.

Walking Lunge

The Walking Lunge is a great pre-workout stretch because it helps to warm up the muscles of your lower back and joints. It also stretches the hamstrings and glutes (buttocks), which are important for proper running form.

Stand with your feet hip-width apart and keep your hands locked together. Take a step forward with one foot, bend both knees until your back knee nearly touches the ground, then step forward again with that same foot and repeat on the other side. Walk down into each lunge until you feel a good stretch in your legs.

Tips: You can perform walking lunges holding dumbbells or barbells in front of you; try holding weights at chest level if you want a more challenging version of this stretch!

Post Workout Stretch Routine

Arm & Wrist Stretch

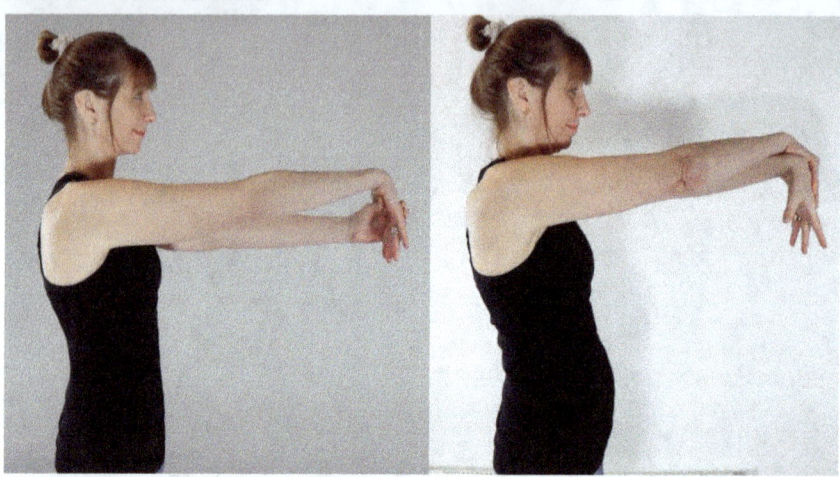

This is a great stretch for the arms and wrists. It is also very easy to do. Start by standing up with your legs shoulder-width apart and stretch your arms in front of you. Do what feels comfortable and bend your hands only as much as your body allows. Hold this position for 30 seconds.

This exercise stretches out all of the muscles in your arms and wrists, which can become tight after doing any kind of exercise involving your hands or arms, such as weight lifting or yoga.

It's important to remember that not all stretches are created equal! A good stretch should be gentle and gradual, not painful or forced. If you feel any pain or discomfort, stop immediately and seek advice from your doctor or physical therapist before continuing any of these stretches.

Seated Spinal Twist

The Seated Spinal Twist is a great pose to do after a workout. It will help you stretch out your back, hips, and shoulders while also calming your mind. This pose is very similar to the Yoga Hero Pose, but with one important difference: The hand position.

To perform this stretch, sit on the floor with your legs crossed and reach one arm behind you with both hands on the floor. Twist toward one side, then the other side. Repeat this 3-5 times on each side.

Standing Quadricep Stretch

The standing quadriceps stretch is a great way to increase flexibility in your quadriceps, hamstrings, and glutes. This stretch is most effective when done after a workout or other activity that causes tightness in your legs.

The standing quadricep stretch is a great way to stretch the front of your thighs and hips. This stretch can help relieve tightness in the front of your leg after performing exercises such as squats and lunges.

Stand with one foot and hold the other one with your corresponding hand. Pull the foot with your hand until it reaches your buttock. Bend your front knee until you feel a stretch in front of that thigh - hold for 20 seconds. Switch sides and

repeat on the other side.

Butterfly

The butterfly stretch helps to loosen up your hip flexors and groin area, which are often tight after running or other activities that involve repetitive hip movements.

Lie on your back with your knees bent and feet flat on the floor. Bring one knee up so that it's straight and pointing toward the ceiling, but don't lock it out at the knee joint. Be sure to keep this knee over your ankle so that you don't hyperextend your knee joint.

Reach across your body with both hands and grab onto the top of your bent knee (as if you were pulling it toward yourself). You can use a towel or strap if you find it difficult to hold onto your leg without falling off balance during this exercise!

Keeping your shoulders flat on the floor, pull gently on the knee while simultaneously pushing out against it with your foot on the floor until you feel the tension in your groin muscles. Hold this position for 3-5 seconds before releasing and repeating on the opposite side.

Cobra Pose

The cobra pose is great for stretching and relaxing your whole body. It's an easy pose to do, but it's also very effective at opening up your chest, shoulders, and upper back. It can be done after a workout or anytime you need to unwind from the day.

To get into the cobra position, lie on your stomach with your legs together and arms by your sides. Slowly raise your upper body off the floor, moving at a comfortable pace that does not cause pain or strain in your lower back. You can support yourself on your forearms if needed. Hold for several deep breaths before lowering yourself down again slowly and gently.

Child's Pose

The Child's Pose is a gentle stretch that anyone can perform, regardless of age, fitness level, or flexibility. It can help relieve lower back pain and fatigue while improving posture and circulation. This pose is especially beneficial for runners as it helps to release tight hip flexors and hamstrings.

Morning Stretch Routine

Knees-to-Chest Stretch

The Knees-to-Chest Stretch is a great way to stretch your hip flexors after you have woken up. To perform this stretch, lie on your back and bring one or both knees up toward your chest. You should feel the stretch in the front of your hip. Hold the position for 15 to 30 seconds, and then switch legs. You can repeat this stretch two or three times on each side.

The Knees-to-Chest Stretch targets the iliopsoas muscle, which runs from the top of the pelvis to the thigh bone (femur). The iliopsoas help you raise your legs when you walk or run, and they assist with sitting upright from a reclining position. This muscle can become tight after sitting for long periods of time without moving around much, such as during sleep.

Glute Bridge

This exercise stretches out your glutes and prepares them for whatever demands are placed on them during the day. It also helps increase blood flow to your muscles so that they can recover after a long night's rest.

To perform this exercise, lie on your back with your hands behind your head, knees bent at 90 degrees, and feet flat on the floor (you can also use an exercise mat). Now push through your heels and raise your buttock off of the floor until it's fully extended. Hold this position for up to 30 seconds before lowering back down slowly.

Seated Oblique Stretch

This stretch is great for the morning and will help improve your hips, shoulders, and torso flexibility. This will make you more mobile throughout the day, which will allow you to perform better in your daily activities. The Seated Oblique Stretch also helps to improve blood flow and increase flexibility in the spine and hips.

Start by lying down. Lean forward at the waist until you feel the tension in your obliques (the muscles on either side of your abdomen). Slowly lean further forward until you feel a deep stretch along your trunk. Hold this position for 20 seconds before releasing and repeating on the opposite side.

Supine Butterfly Stretch

The butterfly stretch is a great exercise to use at the beginning of the day. It helps to open up the hips and groin, which can help improve your mobility in these areas. This will also help you get your blood flowing to perform better during your workout. The butterfly stretch is a great way to increase flexibility in the hips, thighs, and groin. It's also a good warm-up before any type of exercise, whether it be yoga or weight lifting.

To do this stretch, start by laying flat on the ground with both feet flat on the floor and your hands resting behind your head with palms facing up. You want to make sure that you're lying on an even surface while placing a towel or a roll underneath your back. Try to keep the back from reaching the rolled towel and curving the muscles as much as your body allows.

Make sure that your knees are bent at 90 degrees and your feet are together as much as possible while still keeping them flat on the floor. Hold for about 5-10 seconds, then release.

Supine Twist Stretch

This exercise stretches the spine, shoulders, and hips. It also helps to release tension from the chest, upper back, and abdominal muscles.

Sit on the floor with your knees bent and crossed with each other (like shown in the picture). Place your hands behind your bent knee and twist your body slowly. Inhale as you twist to the right side, bringing your right elbow toward the left knee and rotating through your midsection. Exhale as you return to the center and repeat on the other side.

Neck Stretch

Neck stretches are a great way to warm up your muscles and joints. They can also be performed at any time during your day for added flexibility and joint health. You can't just move your head around to get a good stretch. You have to be in the right position.

The best way to do this is by getting down on your hands and knees or sitting on a chair with your back straight. Then you can use both hands to gently pull your head toward one shoulder and then the other. You should feel a deep stretch in the neck muscle on each side of your head, and you should also feel some tightness in the middle of your back and shoulders as well as along the sides of your body.

Cat-Cow

The cat and cow pose is a great way to wake up your body, and it helps loosen up your hips and spine, which can help prevent injury throughout the day. Start on all fours with your hands directly under your shoulders, knees directly under your hips, and wrists directly beneath your shoulders. Spread your fingers wide apart and press into the floor with them for stability.

On an inhale, lift your head, chest and tailbone up toward the ceiling as you round the back like an angry cat arching its back in preparation to pounce on its prey. Tuck in the chin slightly so you don't strain your neck by over-extending it while arching backward.

Hold this position for 5 breaths, then exhale as you slowly go back down into Cow Pose while simultaneously pressing forward with both hands until they are flat against the ground in front of you. Your spine should be relaxed throughout both movements. Hold this position for 5 more breaths, then repeat on each side 2 more times each.

Mountain Pose

The mountain pose stretch is a great way to loosen up your lower back, hips, and legs in the morning. It also helps you center yourself mentally so you can focus on daily tasks ahead.

Stand with your feet hip-width apart, toes pointing forward or slightly turned out. Bring your hands together at chest level in front of your heart center. Exhale as you lift through the crown of your head, elongating the spine and lifting into an arched back. Hold for three deep breaths. Repeat once more if desired.

Nighttime stretch routine

Neck stretches

The neck is one of the most sensitive parts of the body. It's very easy to get a stiff neck from poor posture and sitting on your couch for too long. This is a great stretch for beginners because you don't have to worry about balance or coordination. You can do this stretch while watching TV or even sitting on your bed before sleep!

Sit up straight and comfortably, with your back against a wall or couch. Make sure you're not slouching or rounding your back forward. Rotate your neck in different positions and stretch it at different angles. That's it! You should feel instant relief in tension around your neck and shoulders!

Bear hug

The bear hug stretch is a stretch that helps with shoulder pain. It can also help to improve mobility in the back and shoulders, which are two areas that commonly experience tightness due to sitting all day.

Start by lying down with your feet shoulder-width apart, knees bent, and arms in front of you. Then pretend you are giving yourself a tight hug by crossing your arms over your chest and reaching your back with the tip of your fingers. Hold for 30 seconds and repeat 2 times.

Reclining bound angle pose

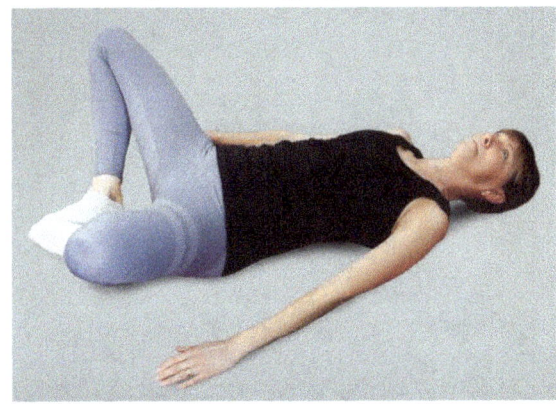

If you're having trouble falling asleep, this pose can help relieve stress and tension in your body. As you exhale, lengthen your spine and rest your head on a cushion or block. If you have any shoulder pain, place a blanket underneath your shoulder blades to take some of the pressure off your neck. This pose is also good for people with high blood pressure or insomnia.

Sit on the floor and bring your legs together. Bend your knees, placing the soles of your feet flat on the floor so that they are hip-width apart. Press down into your feet as you lift your waist up.

Seated forward bend

This is a great stretch for nighttime. You can do it before bed to help relax the body, but you can also do it in the morning when you wake up to help release tension from your body.

The seated forward bend is one of the most basic stretches. It's great for beginners because it's a gentle way to get into a deeper stretch, but also great for advanced yogis because many variations can be done with this pose.

For this version of the seated forward bend, you need to get into the pose from a seated position. Once you're comfortable in the pose, bend forward while reaching for your legs. Make sure to always keep your eyes on the horizon line so that your neck doesn't become strained during any of these poses.

Child's pose

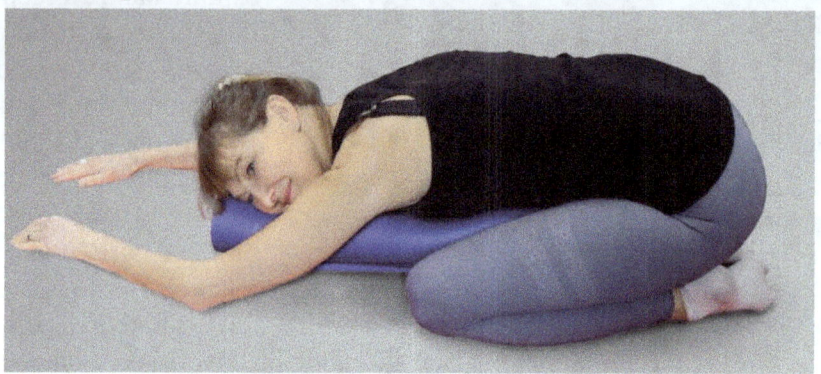

This stretch is perfect for those suffering from insomnia. It stretches your hips, shoulders, and neck. It also helps you relax before bed. The child's pose is a great yoga pose for stretching your hips and back. It can help relieve tension in the lower back and hamstrings, improve circulation and reduce stress.

As an older adult, there are some considerations that you should keep in mind when stretching. For example, if you have osteoporosis or arthritis, you must talk to your doctor before starting this type of program. Also, if you have any type of cardiovascular disease, it's best to talk to your doctor before attempting any type of physical activity.

If you start feeling any type of discomfort or pain when practicing these stretches, then you can skip it and continue stretching another area of the body. Listening to your body will help you remain safe and get better results!

Diet

If you're serious about getting the most out of your stretching routine, it's important to know which exercises are best for you and what foods will support those efforts. If you're trying to improve flexibility, you need to ensure that your diet provides the nutrients and fuel you need for your body to recover from workouts and perform at its best.

Many people think eating a high-protein diet will help them become more flexible. That's not necessarily the case. While protein is important for building muscle, you don't need an excess of protein in your diet to increase flexibility. If you eat too much protein, it could make your muscles tighter and less flexible.

You should also be mindful of what types of foods you're eating. Some foods are easier to digest than others, which means they provide more energy; eating them before exercise and stretches can help you stay energized longer. However, some foods can cause indigestion or gas (or both), which can lead to cramps or discomfort while stretching or exercising.

Food is fuel, and it's important to eat well. But if you're an older adult, you must nourish your body with a nutritious diet. Eating right helps keep your body strong and healthy as you age. It also helps prevent certain diseases, such as heart disease and diabetes. As the body ages, it also becomes more difficult to lose weight.

Also, the most common cause of weight gain in the elderly is the loss of muscle mass. As you age, your body doesn't work as well to keep you active and burn calories. You may also find it harder to move around and may not want to do so as much. The second most common cause of weight gain in the elderly is a decline in metabolic rate.

This happens because your body just doesn't burn as many calories when it's not getting enough nutrients or oxygen-rich blood. Even if you don't gain any weight, these changes alone can make you feel more tired and less energetic.

A study from the University of Copenhagen found that as people age, the bacterial population in their gut changes significantly. This change can lead to a lack of nutrients being absorbed. The most common cause is an increase in inflammation in the gut due to things such as stress and chronic dieting.

It also causes other problems, including digestive issues like bloating and constipation. The bacteria in our guts help us digest foods by producing enzymes that break down certain carbs and fats into smaller molecules that are easier for our bodies to use as energy or store as fat tissue. Without enough good bacteria, you may struggle to digest certain foods like dairy or gluten-containing grains that give most people no issues at all.

Due to age, the digestive tract is not as efficient as it once was. Another reason why the digestive tract is affected by aging is actually from other health conditions that may be present, along with the medication that deals with those conditions:

- Diabetes can affect the ability to digest foods
- Heartburn medications can affect how well you absorb nutrients
- High blood pressure medications can affect the absorption of vitamins and minerals
- Some types of arthritis medications can increase your risk of developing gallstones or pancreatitis if you don't eat enough fiber in your diet

Other things that may affect your digestion include changes in hormones such as menopause or andropause (male menopause), medications such as steroids, lack of exercise, or poor posture, which can contribute to acid reflux and heartburn.

The mucus lining in the stomach protects against stomach acid, for example, and the small intestine helps to filter bacteria out of food before it enters your bloodstream.

But as you age, these and other protective mechanisms that help prevent damage to your digestive system may be less effective than they once were – which is one reason older adults often feel more intestinal discomfort from foods that didn't bother them when they were younger.

Here are some ways age affects digestion:

1. The mucus lining in your stomach becomes thinner as you age, so it's less effective at protecting against stomach acid. That makes it easier for bacteria to enter the bloodstream through a cut or scratch in your stomach lining – which can lead to infection or inflammation elsewhere in the body.
2. Your small intestine doesn't have as much bile production as it once did, so nutrients aren't absorbed as efficiently from foods like fat and protein. That leads to a condition

called malabsorption syndrome – which can cause problems such as diarrhea or constipation and weight loss

The following tips will help you choose foods to protect digestion as you age:

Eat more plant-based foods. Plant-based foods are rich in fiber, vitamins, and minerals, and they also contain less saturated fat than animal products. The term "fiber" refers to the material that makes up plants. This indigestible material is found in all plant foods, including fruits, vegetables, and whole grains. The difference between fiber and other carbohydrates is that fiber cannot be digested by the body. Instead of being absorbed into your bloodstream like other carbs, fiber passes through your digestive system unchanged.

Fiber helps maintain bowel health by keeping waste moving through your colon smoothly. This can help prevent constipation and diverticular disease (a painful condition of the bowel). It may help lower cholesterol levels in your blood by slowing the absorption of fat from food in the intestines.

Low-density lipoprotein cholesterol is often referred to as "bad" cholesterol because it puts you at risk for heart disease if it builds up on artery walls. Fiber doesn't affect high-density lipoprotein cholesterol – known as "good" cholesterol. If you're unsure where to start, try eating more fruits, vegetables, and beans.

Choose low-fat dairy products. Low-fat dairy products such as yogurt, milk, and cheese are good sources of calcium, which helps build strong bones and teeth in adults over the age of 50. They also contain vitamin D, which helps absorb calcium – but if you drink fortified milk or eat fortified cereal regularly, you may not need as much dietary calcium from dairy products.

Low-fat dairy products can help prevent constipation, according to the National Digestive Diseases Information Clearinghouse of the National Institutes of Health. Calcium, magnesium, and phosphorus in dairy products help with the regulation of bowel movements by increasing stool frequency and consistency. Low-fat dairy products are also high in potassium which helps reduce the risk of kidney stones.

Choose meat with no added fat or salt (look for "loin" cuts). Lean cuts of meat are rich in protein but have little or no saturated fat or cholesterol – two factors that can increase your risk for heart disease if you eat too much of them during middle age or later years. Also, limit red meat to no more than once a week if possible because it's high in saturated fat and may increase your risk of colon cancer if consumed regularly.

The American Heart Association recommends eating less than 10 percent of calories from saturated fat and less than 300 mg per day of dietary cholesterol. Saturated fat raises blood cholesterol levels, increasing your chance of developing heart disease.

Because meat is high in protein, iron, and zinc – all nutrients needed for strength – it should be part of every person's diet. But you'll want to make sure it has no added fat or salt, so it doesn't cause stomach upset or other digestive problems. Lean cuts of beef include tenderloin, top loin, and sirloin. Lean pork cuts include tenderloin and top loin. Skinless chicken breast and turkey breast are also good choices for reducing fat and calories.

Choose whole grains instead of refined carbohydrates. Whole grains contain more nutrients than refined grains, such as white bread and rice cakes, because they haven't been stripped of their nutritional value during processing. Whole grains are also easier on the digestive system than refined grains because they contain more fiber – the indigestible part of plants that helps food pass through your intestines without causing bloating or constipation.

Drinking water frequently helps with digestion. Drinking water helps flush out waste products from your body, such as toxins, bacteria, and food residue. It also helps to prevent constipation by keeping your colon healthy and moving waste through your body at a normal rate. In addition to helping with digestion, drinking water also keeps your skin looking younger because it keeps you hydrated.

Water is essential for survival because it makes up 60 percent of the human body. According to the National Health Service, the average adult needs about 1 milliliter of water per calorie consumed each day to avoid dehydration symptoms like headaches, fatigue, weakness, and dizziness.

Consistency

It can be hard to stay consistent when you're trying to make a change in your life. Sometimes we lose patience, our resolve weakens, or we just don't know what to do next. But if you want to create lasting change, consistency is key. When it comes to stretching, many things can stop you from doing it regularly.

For example, you may have a busy schedule or lack the motivation to stretch. Or, maybe you're just too tired and need a break. But if you want to stick with your stretching routine, you need to make some changes in your life so that stretching becomes easier.

Identify your motivations

What's driving you? Is it an event that happened recently? Is it something you want for yourself or someone else? When you're trying to figure out what motivates you to stretch, it's important to take a step back and evaluate why you want to do it.

It's easy to get caught up in the excitement of something new, but it's important to make sure that you're stretching and putting your body through a positive change for all the right reasons. Once you know what's driving you, write it down or memorize it so that you can remind yourself why this is important to you when you feel like quitting.

Focus on progress, not perfection

People who get results don't focus on getting everything right all at once; they focus on getting better every day and celebrating their small victories. Perfectionism is a paralyzing force. It stops us from taking action or making progress because we're afraid we won't be able to do it perfectly. But perfectionism is an illusion - nothing can be done perfectly. Trying to do so only leads to frustration and burnout.

It's easy to lose sight of what matters most: the big picture. When we focus too much on the small details (like doing the stretch correctly) and we forget about the main focus of why we are doing it in the first place, it's easy to lose perspective and feel hopeless about our goals.

As a result of this mindset, many people stop exercising, stretching, or improving their life altogether when things don't go their way. To avoid this trap, try setting aside time each day to reflect on your progress - not how well you performed but how far you've come since yesterday, last week, or last month!

Create a routine

Stretch at the same time each day. That way, it becomes part of your normal routine - like eating breakfast or brushing your teeth - instead of something extra you have to do at an inconvenient time.

Having a routine can help you stay on track with your goals, save time and energy, and reduce stress. Routine also makes decision-making easier because it reduces the number of choices you have to make each day.

You'll be more likely to follow through on your plans if you know exactly what you need to do next. A good routine lets you plan out every step in advance so that when it's time to stretch your body, all you need to do is follow the program. For example:

If I want to start stretching at 6 pm every day, then schedule that appointment with yourself first thing in the morning when you are fresh and motivated.

Make it fun

There are many ways to make stretching more fun, so you're more likely to stick with it.

Use music as a distraction. Try listening to music while you stretch, or turn on some upbeat tunes that get you moving. You'll be less likely to notice how long you're stretching if you're having fun!

Challenge yourself with new moves. If you've been doing the same stretches for some time, try something new and see what happens! A little variety can help keep things interesting and keep your body guessing - so it won't know what's coming next!

Sign up for a class. If you're a senior, there are many reasons why you should consider signing up for a local stretching class. Consider signing up for a local class offered by your community center or gym. If there isn't a class available in your area, look for an online program that offers virtual stretching classes.

If you are interested in yoga and want to try it out, there are some things to consider before signing up for a local yoga class offered by your community center or gym. It's important to remember that you may be more fragile than your younger counterparts.

The following are some considerations you should take into account when choosing a class:

- The teacher should be experienced in teaching seniors. They should also be aware of any special needs you might have.
- The studio or gym should have adequate lighting and space for movement.
- There shouldn't be too much noise from other participants or loud music playing in the background that could distract from the lesson.
- It's always better to start with beginner classes, so you don't get overwhelmed by an advanced class with fast-paced movements.

The end results

You're just beginning a stretching program, wondering if you'll see results immediately. The answer depends on how much stretching you do and how consistent you are with it. Stretching is one of the most important parts of any exercise program.

If you've never stretched before or haven't done it regularly for a long time, it will take some time to get back into shape. That said, if you're consistent with your stretching routine, you might see the first results in about six weeks or even less.

Stretching programs can offer a wide range of benefits, including improved flexibility, decreased muscle soreness, and injury prevention. However, it's important to remember that the benefits of stretching are cumulative and don't occur overnight.

Most people see results after just a few weeks of consistent stretching. If you're not seeing any improvement after six weeks, try increasing your time or frequency of stretching. The best way to ensure your muscles stay flexible is to stretch every day or at least three times per week.

After all, if you don't use it, you lose it!

Here's another book by Scott Hamrick that you might like

Free Bonuses from Scott Hamrick

Hi seniors!

My name is Scott Hamrick, and first off, I want to THANK YOU for reading my book.

Now you have a chance to join my exclusive "workout for seniors" email list so you can get the ebook below for free as well as the potential to get more ebooks for seniors for free! Simply click the link below to join.

P.S. Remember that it's 100% free to join the list.

Access your free bonuses here
https://livetolearn.lpages.co/scott-hamrick-stretching-for-seniors-paperback/